Gilli Davies is a cooke
guest appearances on
weekly column for th

LAMB, LEEKS AND LAVERBREAD

The Best of Welsh Cookery

GILLI DAVIES

GRAFTON BOOKS

A Division of the Collins Publishing Group

LONDON GLASGOW
TORONTO SYDNEY AUCKLAND

Grafton Books
A Division of the Collins Publishing Group
8 Grafton Street, London W1X 3LA

A Grafton Paperback Original 1989

ISBN 0-586-20139-4

Printed and bound in Great Britain by
Collins, Glasgow

Set in Palatino

CONTENTS

Acknowledgements	7
Introduction	9
Love Spoons	16
Cookery Skills	17
Notes on the Recipes	23
First Courses and Light Meals	25
Fish	69
Poultry and Game	115
Meat	151
Dishes without Meat	197
Puddings	237
Baking	273
Drinks and Preserves	307
Wild Wales	323
Welsh Cheeses	326
Index	332

ACKNOWLEDGEMENTS

Compiling and writing this book of Welsh food has been a pleasure. Travelling through Wales I have met some delightful people, and hope that those who have worked with me in the collection of material have enjoyed the project as much as I have.

In particular I should like to thank Minwel Tibbott, Roger Worsley, Nerys Curig, Alan Mackay, Richard Wilford, Kemmis Buckley, Eleri Evans, Lynda Kettle, Jean-Pierre and Jan Mifsud, Merion and Pat Dally, and Eluned Lloyd with her gastronomic guesthouse.

For the photos, many thanks to Perry Photographics Consultants Limited and the National Museum of Wales (Welsh Folk Museum), who also provided the sketch of the love spoon.

Enormous thanks to the Welsh Development Agency who gave me their time and space to assemble my research, the National Museum of Wales (Welsh Folk Museum) again, for a glimpse of Wales past, Cardiff Central Library – and Bryn in particular for his patience – and British Gas plc Wales for their collection of authentic recipes.

The greatest accolade must go to the second-year HND students of the Cardiff Institute of Higher Education. Under the skilled leadership of Les Hart these cooks from the Catering Department have tried, tested and remarked on each and every recipe . . . and lived to read the finished book!

Grateful acknowledgement is made to the following for their kind permission to reprint copyright material:

B. T. Batsford Ltd for extracts from *Welsh Country Upbringing* by David Parry-Jones

Bobby Freeman for an extract from her book *First Catch Your Peacock* (Image Imprint)

Gomer Press for extracts from *Give Me Yesterday* by James Williams

Michael Joseph Ltd for extracts from *How Green Was My Valley* by Richard Llewellyn

INTRODUCTION

Lamb, Leeks and Laverbread –
Is there more to Welsh Food?

Yes, indeed there is and I look forward to introducing you through this book to the wealth of fine recipes which can be found in Wales today. Visitors to the principality will already know our Celtic connections, how we like to stew food in a pot, bake on a griddlestone, and eat that healthy but extraordinary seaweed. But there is more, much much more to be discovered in Wales in culinary terms.

To begin with it is worth examining how the Welsh have eaten over the centuries. A good place to start is with the daffodil. These were introduced by the Romans as food rather than decoration, eaten as a stimulating pudding with beaten green figs. Fish were so popular with the Romans that they imported their own fennel, coriander, lovage, fenugreek, rue, dill, pennyroyal, tansy, savory, mustard seed and thyme to flavour the multitude of fish caught in the rivers and off the Welsh coasts. They adored prawns, scallops and oysters, even cockles and seaweed, all of which they found in abundance in Wales. The Romans also planted vines for their wine, and those same south-facing slopes in the more sheltered regions of Gwent, Glamorgan and Dyfed in South Wales still produce grapes for a limited vine harvest enjoyed by the lucky few. Wild garlic plants, or ramsons, which grow so prolifically around the coasts and in damp woodland areas, have been here since Roman times. In fact Ramsey Island on the south-west tip is named after them. Another island, Bardsey, was the birthplace of Welsh whisky as long ago as the 4th century A.D. It is believed that Renault Hir of Bardsey obtained the formula for distilling whisky from visiting merchants, and there is a Welsh whisky company in existence today.

In the 12th century Giraldus Cambrensis (Gerald the Welsh)

wrote extensively of life in Wales during his travels with
Baldwin, archbishop of Canterbury, and described the diet thus:
'Almost all the population lives on its flocks and on oats, milk,
cheese and butter.' And of course they did live off the land.
Wales was, and for the most part still is, a pastoral country,
with good soil, a mild climate from the Gulf Stream and a
tradition of farming. Oats were the main cereal crop and during
the 16th century water mills appeared throughout Wales –
situated wherever the torrent of a fast-flowing river could be
utilized – to mill oats, barley, and later wheat. It was normal
practice for each farmer to barter with the miller for his services,
exchanging milling for some of the milled flour. Animal husbandry of pigs, lamb and cattle was common. Since a farmer's
status depended on the size of his cattle herd few cows were
slaughtered, and the farmer's wife used all the milk she could
in the dairy. Cheese, cream and buttermilk were plentiful and
cooking based on milk has become part of the tradition of Welsh
food. Buttermilk was and still is used in much of Welsh baking
and it makes a delicious addition to cooked root vegetables.

The central feature of the Celtic kitchen has always been the
open hearth which supplied direct heat to cook over. The main
meal of the day was cawl, a stew cooked in one large pot
suspended over the fire. It consisted of meat – either pork, beef
or lamb – which was boiled until tender, with the addition of
root vegetables, herbs and sometimes oats to thicken the stew.
Often the meat would provide one meal and the remaining
vegetables and soup could feed the family on another occasion.

The other mainstay of Celtic cuisine was the bakestone or
griddle. This flat iron disc of about 45 cm (18 in) diameter was
heated over the embers of the fire then used to cook dough or
batters. The griddle is found extensively throughout the Celtic
countries – Wales, Scotland, Ireland and Brittany – and pancakes and oatcakes are common to each region, although the
crispness of a crêpe can hardly be compared with a thick,
currant-filled Welsh pancake. Lloyd George loved them stacked
high and soaked in butter for his tea.

This diet of soup and griddle cakes may sound dull, but it
was certainly nourishing and was enlivened by the constant
supply of fresh fish and dairy products; even the hedgerows

could be plundered for crops of berries and fruit. Meat, fish and even cheese were pickled, cured and smoked so they could be kept through the winter. Just imagine a cottage in rural Wales with the chimney place full of hanging hams. These might well have been hams of mutton rather than pork, and were often supplemented by smoked mackerel or herring from the sea as well as a Caerphilly cheese tucked away in a nook or cranny. The larder would be well stocked with preserves, bottled fruit and vegetables, to say nothing of the wines made throughout the year and often more potent than one might imagine.

If you have the chance to visit The Welsh Folk Museum at St Fagans, just outside Cardiff in South Wales, you will be lucky enough to see the reconstruction of this very basic cooking style in some of the cottages. The museum is a must for anyone interested in the history of Welsh food.

One of the major contributors to the study of Welsh cookery was a 19th-century English woman, Lady Augusta Hall, who later became Lady Llanover. Wife of the MP Benjamin Hall of Abergavenny, she worked zealously to revive and improve Welsh culture. She was a formidable lady who not only learnt the Welsh language, painted well, and created a small textile factory but also wrote extensively. Her book *Good Cookery* (1867) combines a fictional story with some excellent recipes using Welsh produce, such as salt duck, or salmon with Teifi sauce. Her description of a Welsh flock of sheep makes fascinating reading as her knowledge of farming was extremely good for a woman at that time. Alas, her efforts to curb the alcohol intake of her neighbours by buying and then closing all the local inns put her out of favour a little!

Lady Llanover perceived one of the great strengths of the Welsh – their hospitality. She wrote of a visitor to Wales, 'Hospitality had greeted him and courtesy had taken him prisoner.' Sometimes described as a nation who are backwards in coming forwards the Welsh on the whole are not bold, almost shy, and yet these gentle people with their soft, lilting accent delight in entertaining.

Giraldus, journeying through Wales to preach a crusade in 1188, also praised the Welsh for their kindness in welcoming strangers and guests: 'No one of this nation ever begs, for the houses of all are common to all; and they consider liberality and hospitality amongst the first virtues.' He described how a family, however poor, would offer the first slice cut from any loaf to a passing traveller. At that time in Wales diners would sit three at a table in order to make friends and gather maximum gossip. After a while they would rotate and make up another threesome. Meanwhile the food was served in large trenchers or bowls, and songs were sung to the harp. The fare may have been very simple, with broth and bread, but at least the welcome was genuine.

Think of the Welsh dresser, taking pride of place in any kitchen, a fine piece of furniture stacked with plates, cutlery and food in readiness to entertain visitors. And in those bygone days before easy transport when, in the turbulent landscape of Wales, a remote farm might see few visitors, any traveller was guaranteed a warm welcome and a table laid in his honour. Bakestone cakes could be rustled up in a jiffy to offer the guest, and *teisennau tincer* (tinker's cakes) is just this kind of recipe, for a travelling tinker must have been given quite a welcome.

Many traditional Welsh recipes (some of which appear in this book) have their roots buried in seasonal events – harvest broth and harvest cake, threshing cake, shearing cakes, Llanddarog Fair cakes, Michaelmas cawl, Fairing pies, Templeton Fair Katt Pies and so on. However, many recipes for festive and even everyday dishes differ from one valley to another. Each region, if not square mile, in Wales boasts a different recipe for cawl, and likewise every community cooks a different cake for customs and celebrations. The biggest divide must be between the north and south of Wales whose diet and dialect differ considerably. But just by looking at a map of Wales one can see that logistically recipes can travel more easily from east to west, than from north to south.

The national emblems of Wales are, of course, the leek and the daffodil. David, our patron saint for whom we sing so lustily on 1 March, is reputed to have fed on the leeks that he gathered in the fields. Welshmen wore leeks at the battle of Heathfield in 633 A.D. when fighting against the Saxon invaders and in medieval times at the battle of Crecy. Henry Tudor is said to have chosen the leek for his emblem because the colours corresponded with his coat of arms of Valois. In Tudor times presents of leeks were given to the royal family by soldiers coming from Wales. Nowadays the leek is most in evidence when it appears in giant form at rugby matches. Luckily we no longer eat daffodils and their fresh yellow colour brings a touch of spring to St David's Day.

Many of the ancient culinary customs survive. However, this book aims to show not only how such customs have been adapted to suit modern tastes but also how contemporary cooks are continuing to use local produce to create new traditions in Welsh cooking. Good, wholesome, even plain food is what the Welsh diet has boasted over the past 200 years. Fine-quality raw materials, simple cooking and healthy appetites – what more could one ask for? Quite a lot it seems, and Wales is taking the changes in its stride without losing the unique character of its cooking.

The huge variety we enjoy in our diet today is due to modern trends and influences. Because of improved methods of transportation and refrigeration we now have access to foods from all over the world, and a new awareness of the relationship between diet and health means that food plays an increasingly significant role in all our lives as we become more discerning about what we eat. Not that the diet rich in dairy fats, animal fats and often refined flour was unsuited to the old rural communities, but life is easier now and we must adjust our diet to our sedentary ways.

So what of the traditional Welsh cooking is still alive in Wales? The best of it, of course. Recipes handed down through the generations for dishes just too good to dismiss, too loved to be forgotten. But even those change and adapt a little to current tastes. Just a spoonful less sugar in the cake, polysunsaturated fat substituted for butter, perhaps, or the fat skimmed off the cawl before serving.

In Wales we are lucky, for we have the best of all foods right here at our fingertips. With a coastline of 750 miles we can boast a superb variety of fish. And now, when the traditions in the fishing industry are combined with efforts to reseed the oyster, mussel and scallop beds, when young lobsters are being reintroduced into the Menai Straits, and crabs are still in abundance on the Welsh rocks, the choice is better than ever before. Rivers are full of salmon and sea trout, with new developments also for both these fish in Milford Haven dock and trout farms to make fishing easy. We have the chance to eat mackerel as it should be eaten, straight from the sea. And don't forget seaweed, so good for you and so good to cook with.

Like the Romans before them the Vikings enjoyed fish, and they named the fishing port of Solva on the west coast of Wales after samphire, the edible seaweed which they found growing there in profusion. Seaweed is still very popular in Wales. Laver (*porphyra umbilicalis*), a lettuce-leaf type of seaweed, is collected daily and boiled in small, family-run factories along the south coast. It is then sold from market stalls and travelling fish vans by the pound in the form of a gelatinous green purée which has, not surprisingly, a faint taste of the sea about it.

Wales is renowned for producing the finest lamb. But don't eat Welsh lamb on 1 March, St David's day, for the valley lambs that are available then have little taste. Wait if you can until autumn when mountain lamb, with its slow-maturing flesh full of flavour, arrives in the butchers'. Look for the new cuts of Welsh lamb, lean as you like and easy to cook.

As for the dairy scene, well, we have Welsh butter, fine milk, and, perhaps most exciting of all, over sixty farmhouse cheeses produced with skill and care throughout Wales. Full of character and flavour, local cheeses are worth seeking out next time you visit Wales.

Don't forget to make the most of wild Wales and pick handfuls of berries from the hedgerows – whinberries, gooseberries, blackberries, tayberries, raspberries and others. Wild mushrooms thrive on the vast expanses of uncultivated woodland in Wales, as do wild herbs, garlic, and so many more exciting and delicious things. Pick your own samphire or laver from the seashore, collect mussels, cockles, winkles and razor shells. Make your own mead from Welsh honey, brew country wine as has been done for so many generations in rural Wales, or buy it from one of the half dozen vineyards in South Wales. Make the fruit into jams, jellies, preserves or pickles or give your health a treat and dine on a wide selection of organically grown vegetables.

Baking has always been a strength of the Celts. Sniff out a good bakery and home in on a loaf of crusty bread, a slice of Bara Brith or some delicious Welsh cakes. Visit one of the weekly markets to collect griddle cakes hot from the bakestone or pick up a bag of fresh cockles. Find some faggots, still made in Wales in the traditional way, on sale every day of the year.

Inspiration for this book has come from a new generation of highly trained and talented chefs. They have given fresh identity to Welsh food by producing superb quality meals from local ingredients, using contemporary cooking skills. Local fishermen supply hotels and restaurants direct, butchers join forces with specialist meat producers, fresh and unusual vegetables are cultivated to meet the growing national demand and there has been a renaissance in the production of a large variety of farmhouse cheeses.

Travelling through Wales I am constantly amazed and delighted by the choice of local dishes and the inspiration of their tastes. There is no longer any need for luxuries to be imported from afar, for we have all that we need in Wales. How much fresher local crab and home-grown fennel must be than imported langoustine and mangetout, so let's eat Welsh produce and revel in its freshness.

With the accent on combining good traditional fare with modern, healthier cooking methods I hope that my selection of recipes will give you an insight into food in Wales today. May I encourage you to explore the depths of the Welsh countryside, comb the seashore and visit the specialist restaurants. If you don't have the opportunity to visit, then perhaps I can inspire you to try a taste of Wales through my recipes, using the ingredients available to you wherever you are.

To quote from Richard Llewellyn in *How Green Was My Valley*, 'If there is better food in Heaven, I am in a hurry to be there.'

Love Spoons

Giving love spoons as tokens of affection is a custom that dates back to the 17th century.

Although the custom can be traced back to German origin, love spoons are peculiar to Wales. Just imagine how many a long winter's evening was whiled away carving a spoon out of wood for the one you loved.

The Welsh Folk Museum at St Fagans has a superb collection, and some of these love spoons have extremely intricate designs, whilst others are quite simple, but most have somewhere the initials of the lovers entwined in the woodwork.

If the more complicated the design the more ardent the love, then you can assume that the love spoon I have adopted as my chapter motif is a declaration of the deepest passion.

Cookery Skills

In this book of Welsh food I aim to inspire the reader to try all the recipes, enthuse over the flavours as I do, and enjoy cooking each dish in the knowledge that it will work. To this end, I hope that you will read this general chapter before you begin cooking. There are a few cookery procedures that tend to baffle most amateur cooks. Don't gasp if I suggest boning a trout, portioning a chicken or chining a rack of lamb. If you follow the instructions below on how to perform these basic tasks you will be able to produce better meals with ease.

Should you live too far away to have the opportunity to buy our fine Welsh foods, don't worry; find a substitute in your region, but do always try to buy fresh, top quality produce. For it is the freshness of the vegetables that makes or mars a good casserole, the full flavour of a farmhouse cheese that adds so much tang to a cheesy dish, and the healthy appearance of fish and meat that gives the meal appeal for the eater.

To joint a chicken
Chicken portions are easy to store in the freezer and simple to cook. But they are by no means the cheapest way to buy chicken. If you buy a large whole bird not only do you get four joints, but the breast as well and the giblets and carcass to make into stock. Buy fresh chicken whenever possible for better flavour and texture. Faced with a whole bird, here's how to dissect it:

A small bird can be halved by placing it, back down, on a board and cutting with a sharp knife or kitchen scissors lengthways down and through the breastbone and then through the backbone. Each half can be further divided into two. Tuck the blade of the knife underneath the leg joint and slice this away from the wing portion, holding the knife at an angle of 45 degrees.

To joint a chicken weighing 1.35 kg (3 lb) or more, first pull the legs away from the body and slice down to where the thigh joins the carcass. Twist the leg around so that the ball and socket joint separates from the carcass. A large leg joint can be divided into the drumstick and thigh. Next, cut down from the breast towards the wing joint, not taking too much breast with it, and sever the wing from the body. With scissors, cut right round the remaining breast meat through the ribs and across the wishbone. Again with scissors, divide the breast into two or three portions, leaving the flesh on the bone. This should give 6–8 portions from a good-sized chicken.

To bone a round fish such as trout or mackerel
First gut the fish and clean under cold running water. Cut off the head, tail and fins. Open out the split fish and spread it flat, skin side up. Press firmly along the centre back of the fish to loosen the backbone, then turn the fish over. Starting at the head end, ease away the backbone with the tip of the knife, removing at the same time as many of the small bones as possible. The fish can now be folded back into its original shape for stuffing.

To bone a loin and best end of neck of lamb
Use a boning knife throughout, or the sharpest knife you have. Blunt knives need more power to make them cut and are therefore more likely to slip. Place the lamb skin side down in front of you. With the point of the knife cut down beside the rib bones and carefully lift each one free from the meat. Once the ribs are loose at one end but attached at the other to the backbone, loosen the meat around this and scrape it away so that you can lift the whole bone structure off the meat. Now look for a thin semicircle of hard shoulder blade that lies between the layers of meat and fat at the thinner end of the loin. Lastly, pull out the strip of sinew that runs the length of the loin underneath where the backbone lay. The loin is now ready to season, stuff and roll.

To prepare a best end and loin of lamb to roast as a rack
Buy a best end of neck of lamb weighing between 675–900 g (1½ lb–2 lb) for four people. **Skin** the lamb by holding the top layer of skin with your fingers and scraping it away from the fat with a sharp knife. **Chine** the lamb by cutting carefully through the chine bone (spine) just where it meets the ribs so that the cutlets can be cut through and separated after cooking. Take care not to saw right through the eye of the meat. Score the fat with a sharp knife, cutting diagonally across the joint from both top corners.

To crush a clove of garlic
It is a good idea to keep one chopping board especially for chopping garlic, onions and herbs. Peel the clove and chop into small pieces, sprinkle over a pinch of salt and leave for 3 minutes. During this time the salt will break down the fibres in the garlic and release the juices. Then with the blade of a round-edged knife or palette knife press the chopped garlic so that it breaks down into a pulp. This pulp can now be added direct to any dish requiring garlic and will provide a subtle garlic flavour with a greatly reduced aftertaste.

To thicken a sauce
Sauces can be thickened before they are cooked or afterwards just before the dish is served. To thicken a sauce at the beginning of cooking, say, when making a thick gravy in which to cook a stew or casserole, a **roux** is prepared. Fat, in the form of butter, margarine, lard or oil, is melted in a pan, then enough flour is added to absorb the fat and turn the mixture into a thick sauce of 'tomato puree' consistency. To this basic roux liquid, in the form of stock, vegetable juice, milk etc, is added gradually and the sauce is then brought to the boil to thicken it. As a basic guide, combine 25 g (1 oz) melted butter and 25 g (1 oz) plain flour, mix these well and pour on 300 ml (½ pint) of liquid to make a good pouring sauce.

To thicken a sauce at the end of cooking, for example, after stewing fruit or roasting a joint of meat, there are three options. Cornflour and arrowroot are powders which, when mixed with cold water, can be added to the sauce or to the juices from a

roast and will thicken it with boiling. They do, however, give
the finished sauce rather a glutinous look and to avoid this you
can make up **kneaded butter** which is a combination of equal
quantities of butter and flour blended together with a palette
knife to form a firm paste. Add little pieces of this to the boiling
sauce to thicken it and give a rich, glossy finish.

To prepare pastry
Instructions for making a range of different pastries are given in
the following recipes:
SHORTCRUST PASTRY in the recipe for Katt pie on page 191
ROUGH PUFF PASTRY in the recipe for pigeon pie on page
   119
SAVOURY CHOUX PASTRY in the recipe for beef, mushroom
   and herb pie on page 160
SUET PASTRY in the recipe for bacon and leek pudding on
   page 162

To make mayonnaise
By making your own mayonnaise you can adjust the flavour to
suit your own taste. I always use the best ingredients possible,
olive oil and fresh lemon juice for example, and the resulting
flavour is so good that I am always glad I took the trouble to
make it myself.

Makes 150 ml (5 fl oz)

1 egg yolk
pinch of salt
pinch of dry mustard
freshly ground white pepper
150 ml (5 fl oz) virgin olive oil
1 tbsp fresh lemon juice

Extra flavourings:
½ clove of garlic, crushed
   with the salt
1 tsp fresh herbs, chopped
1 tbsp white wine vinegar to
   replace lemon juice
a few drops of Tabasco

Use a bowl and balloon whisk, electric whisk or food processor.
First mix the egg yolk, salt, mustard and pepper, whisk hard

for a minute. Then, drop by drop, add the oil, whisking continuously. When about a quarter of the oil has been added and the mayonnaise looks smooth and glossy pour the remaining oil in a thin continuous stream into the mayonnaise, again whisking all the time. By the time the oil is used up the mayonnaise should be very thick indeed. Now whisk in the lemon juice and any other flavouring you may be using.

If the mayonnaise starts to separate or curdle put it on one side and start again with another egg yolk in a clean bowl. Gradually whisk in the curdled mayonnaise.

Mayonnaise will keep for a week in the fridge if covered completely with clingfilm or foil. It does not freeze satisfactorily.

To peel tomatoes
Put the tomatoes in a heatproof bowl and pour enough boiling water over to completely immerse them. Count slowly to ten and drain off the boiling water, replacing it with cold water to stop the tomatoes cooking. Now take a sharp kitchen knife and pierce the skin. It should peel away easily in large sections.

To cook in a bain-marie
This is a method of cooking using indirect heat. Place the dish of uncooked food inside another larger dish or baking tin and surround with about a 2.5 cm (1 in) depth of water. Cook in a moderate oven (gas 4, 350°, 180°C). As the water heats it will cook the food in the dish but without any risk of it boiling. This method of cooking is suitable for any dish that requires gentle cooking, such as egg custards etc.

Tips on making perfect pancakes
Follow instructions carefully for the batter and sieve if lumpy. Keep one pan just for pancakes if possible. Oil the surface each time before you fry the first of a batch of pancakes but there is no need to add subsequent oil between each one. Don't overheat the pan but use a moderate heat so that the pancakes will cook through evenly; this will make turning them easier. Use as little batter as you can, tilting the pan to let it run over the surface . . . and don't worry if the first pancake is a disaster, practice makes perfect!

To flame
Always heat the alcohol in a small pan before you set it alight.
Once alight take the pan off the heat but let the flame die
naturally, when all the alcohol has been burnt off.

To use gelatine
Empty the gelatine grains into the smallest saucepan that you
have and pour over the given amount of *cold* liquid. Leave the
gelatine to soak in this and after a few minutes it will have
swollen to absorb all the liquid – 12 g (½ oz) gelatine absorbs
4 tbsp water. If you heat it gently (on no account let it boil) the
gelatine will dissolve in less than a minute. You can now pour
the dissolved gelatine into your prepared dish.

To use tinfoil
Did you know that tinfoil works in two different ways? The
shiny side deflects the heat and so lessens the effect of cooking
on food it covers. But the dull side absorbs the heat so food
wrapped inside will cook more quickly.

NOTES ON THE RECIPES

Use either metric or imperial measurements in any one recipe, not both, as the two systems are not exact equivalents.

All recipes serve four unless otherwise stated.

Flour is always plain flour unless otherwise stated.

All spoon measures are level unless otherwise stated.

Suggestions for garnish are included, for whatever the flavour it is true that we 'eat with our eyes'.

At the bottom of each recipe I have included a short note, indicated by the letter M, on the compatability of each dish with microwave cooking. Taking into account the enormous variety of microwave ovens now available I have left cooking details to the reader to compare with the manual of his/her own particular model.

There is also a note, indicated by the letter F, about freezing each dish, which I hope will be useful. Almost every household has a freezer these days and our experience of them grows with the seasons, but if you are too busy to fill yours with fresh fruits in season and stacks of homemade cakes, then make a double quantity of a favourite Welsh dish from this book and freeze some for another day.

Where applicable I have indicated with the letters AP at what stage in the recipe the dish can be prepared in advance and then left. How useful it is when planning a special meal to be able to part-cook some of the dishes. For the working cook, meals often have to be prepared earlier in the day to be finished off just before serving.

OVEN TEMPERATURE GUIDE

	Degrees Fahrenheit	Gas Regulo	Degrees Centigrade
Very slow	240–280	¼–½	115–135
Slow	280–320	1–2	135–160
Warm	320–340	3	160–170
Moderate	340–370	4	170–185
Moderately Hot	370–400	5–6	185–205
Hot	400–440	7	205–225
Very Hot	440–480	8–9	225–250

FIRST COURSES AND
LIGHT MEALS

Mussel pâté
Parsley broth
Sorrel soup
Hot scallop mousse with prawn sauce
Pan-fried prawns with sorrel mayonnaise
Mussel broth
Marinated salmon with honey and mustard
  sauce
Chilled salmon and leek soup
Welsh bouillabaisse
Anglesey eggs
Grapefruit with mead
Deep-fried cockles
Crab and laver parcels
Laverbread cakes with bacon
Leek and potato soup
Sorrel parcels with yogurt cheese and prawns
Granny Griffiths' cawl
Green pancakes
Ceredigion cawl
Marinated herrings with apple and lemon
  yogurt
Parsley pie
Fried goat's cheese with rhubarb sauce

It's always exciting to delve into a new cookery book, and nowhere do you get a better feel for the recipes than with the first course. Not too complicated, using ingredients ready to hand to produce a combination of flavours that trigger those saliva glands. Dishes that look really appetizing. After all, isn't the first course supposed to stimulate the appetite for what is to follow?

Some of the recipes for starters in this chapter would make a perfect lunch, although the quantity may need to be doubled. Light and refreshing, for a smaller appetite prepare two starters and forgo a main course altogether.

Let's set the scene on a dinner party in Wales. The door opens and delicious cooking smells waft out from the kitchen to welcome you, the familiar sweet aroma of roast lamb with a hint of rosemary. Your host ushers you into the warmth of the living room, where a coal fire is glowing in the grate, and sitting on an inviting, chintz-covered sofa, you sip a glass of mulled wine. And then to the dining table, a magnificent rectangle of the same polished oak as the Welsh dresser which dominates the room. Blue and white china decorates the dresser, with large, matching jugs and bowls filling the lower shelves. And on the table in front of you, on the very same china, is your first course – a masterpiece of culinary art. Perhaps warming soup, shellfish, cured salmon, or even a little laverbread. Warm rolls are passed round and glasses filled. A harp sounds gently in the background and just for the moment there is contentment in the Land of our Fathers.

Mussel pâté

Pâté cregyn gleision

Fresh, cooked mussels without their shells are now available from good fishmongers. Sold by the 100 g (¼ lb) they are remarkably good value and save all the bother of cleaning and cooking mounds of mussels at home. The flavour and texture may not be as good as the 'do-it-yourself' variety but they are a great improvement on bottled mussels and the ideal main ingredient in this simple pâté.

225 g (8 oz) fresh, cooked mussels
50 ml (2 fl oz) dry white wine
75 g (3 oz) slightly salted butter
1 medium onion, finely chopped
100 g (4 oz) field mushrooms, chopped
1 clove garlic, crushed with salt

75 g (3 oz) wholemeal breadcrumbs
1 tbsp parsley, chopped
juice of ½ lemon
salt and freshly ground black pepper

To garnish
a handful of mussel shells, with mussels if possible
sprigs of parsley

1. Soak the mussels in the white wine.
2. Meanwhile, melt 25 g (1 oz) of the butter and fry the chopped onion without browning for about 5 minutes over gentle heat. Stir in the chopped mushrooms and crushed garlic, and continue to cook for another 3 minutes or until the dark juices just begin to run out of the mushrooms. Add the remaining butter.
3. When the butter has melted, stir in the breadcrumbs, parsley, mussels and white wine. Bring to the boil, then remove

from the heat, season to taste and add enough lemon juice to give a tang to the flavour but not dominate it.

4. Press the mixture into a lightly buttered small terrine or attractively shaped heatproof bowl, cover with foil, and put the dish in a roasting tin containing 25 cm (1 in) of cold water.

5. Cook in a moderate oven (gas 4, 350°F, 180°C) for 45 minutes. Lift out of the hot water, and weight down. (I usually use a large tin of tomatoes!) Leave the weight on the pâté for 12 hours, in the fridge if possible.

6. Garnish the pâté with the mussel shells and parsley. Either serve in the dish or turn out on to a plate and slice to serve.

M   Suitable for microwave cookery

F   Not suitable – the texture may become very 'wet' if frozen

AP Make the pâté up to 2 days in advance and keep chilled

Parsley broth
Cawl phersli

This pretty soup has a certain depth of flavour due to the addition of Marmite instead of vegetable stock. A great success with children, who love the crunchy pearl barley as much as the Marmite flavour, it is the perfect family lunch. Serve with chunks of fresh bread and butter, or try some crisp cheese biscuits for a change.

25 g (1 oz) butter
3 medium carrots, peeled and diced
2 medium turnips or parsnips, peeled and diced
1.2 l (2 pints) water
1 tsp Marmite
50 g (2 oz) pearl barley

3 leeks, thinly sliced
2 tbsp fresh parsley, chopped
salt and freshly ground black pepper

To garnish
yogurt or cream

1. Melt the butter in a large saucepan. Toss in the carrots and turnips, then lower the heat and leave to cook very gently for 10 minutes, taking care not to let them brown.
2. Meanwhile, boil the water and stir in the Marmite.
3. Add the pearl barley to the carrots and turnips, pour on the Marmite water and bring to the boil. Simmer for 20 minutes.
4. Add the leeks, parsley, and seasoning to taste. Simmer the broth again for 10 minutes to cook the leeks through.
5. Serve the soup in bowls with a spoonful of yogurt or cream swirled in each.

M   Suitable for microwave cookery

F   Can be frozen but it will cause the barley to swell, so it may be necessary to add some more Marmite water after reheating

AP Prepare the entire soup up to the end of stage 4

Sorrel soup
Cawl suran

Sorrel is a wild plant which, due to the lack of cultivation of so much of Wales, still grows in abundance in our fields and hedgerows. Its sharp, acid flavour adds a lovely tang to any number of bland dishes and it can be used raw in salads, made into delicious sauces, or to colour and flavour a superb soup.

50 g (2 oz) butter
1 medium onion, finely
  chopped
1 large potato, peeled and
  diced
2 good handfuls of freshly
  picked sorrel
600 ml (1 pint) milk

600 ml (1 pint) light chicken
  or vegetable stock
salt and freshly ground black
  pepper
lemon juice to taste

To garnish
a good dollop of cream

1. In a large saucepan melt the butter and cook the onion and potato for 5 minutes over gentle heat. Toss in the sorrel leaves, stir for one minute, then pour in all the liquid. Season well and bring to the boil.
2. Simmer the soup for 20 minutes then cool slightly before liquidizing or processing to a smooth purée.
3. Taste the soup carefully before adding lemon juice to sharpen the flavour and more seasoning if necessary. Reheat, and garnish with a swirl of cream just before serving.

M   Suitable for microwave cookery

F   Freezes well; add the cream when reheating

AP Cook the soup in advance; add the cream when reheating

Hot scallop mousse with prawn sauce
Bwyd mor poeth gyda saws corgimychiaid

Try to use fresh scallops whenever you can, for once frozen their texture is never quite so good. I first ate this scrumptious mousse at the Meadowsweet Hotel in Llanrwst, Gwynedd, where the smaller but perhaps tastier Queen scallops were readily available from the local seabeds. Buy them still attached to their shells if possible.

Serves 6

250 g (9 oz) fresh scallops
2 large egg whites
150 ml (5 fl oz) double cream
½ tsp tomato purée
salt and freshly ground white pepper

To garnish
25 g (1 oz) prawns

To serve
Melba toast

For the sauce
25 g (1 oz) butter
25 g (1 oz) flour
150 ml (5 fl oz) fish or chicken stock
1 tbsp dry white wine
150 ml (5 fl oz) double cream
50 g (2 oz) fresh prawns
salt and freshly ground white pepper

1. If the scallops are still on the shell reserve any juices then discard the shells and rinse the fish under the cold tap.
2. In a liquidizer or food processor, blend the scallops to a very smooth paste. Add the egg whites and blend again until smooth and well mixed. Add the double cream and blend for a further 2 minutes until you have a smooth cream. Stir in the purée and a little salt and pepper. Thicken the mixture

by chilling for at least one hour in the fridge, but preferably overnight.

3. For the sauce: gently melt the butter in a saucepan, stir in the flour and blend well. Gradually add the stock and the reserved scallop juices, bring to the boil stirring hard, then add the wine, cream, prawns and seasoning. Simmer for 2 minutes and taste for seasoning before serving.

4. To cook the mousse, butter a 15 cm (6 in) soufflé dish or 6 individual ramekin dishes and place some prawns in the bottom for decoration. Spoon the scallop cream into the prepared dishes and sit them in a baking tray half full of cold water. Bake in a moderate oven (gas 5, 375°F, 190°C) until the mousse is firm to the touch – about 30 minutes for the large mousse, 15 minutes for the ramekins.

5. Turn the mousse out on to a large serving dish or individual plates for the ramekins. Spoon some sauce around the base of the mousse, garnish with the remaining prawns and serve immediately with Melba toast.

• The simplest way to make Melba toast is to cook sliced, crustless white bread in the toaster to a medium brown. As soon as it pops up, lay both slices on a flat surface, one on top of the other so that they don't turn too crisp, and slice through them horizontally to make 4 thin slices of toast. Turn the toasted sides back to back, uncooked sides out, and put these back in the toaster. Take care not to let them burn, just toast until the smoke starts to rise . . . take out immediately, they will be perfect.

M   Stage 4 can be adapted to the microwave, adjust timing accordingly

F   Freezes well; pack the sauce separately

AP Prepare up to the end of stage 3; cover the sauce and reheat at time of serving

Pan-fried prawns with sorrel mayonnaise
Corgimychiaid mewn saws suran

'Before the War, prawns, really large prawns as big as your hand, were so numerous amongst the catch that they were thrown overboard lest they waste the fishermen's time,' the wife of a retired trawlerman told me.

Large Dublin Bay prawns are still caught from Milford Haven port, but you have to be keen to catch them as they leave the fishing boats for they are immediately transported to France. Knowing a fisherman is the only sure way to guarantee a supply of these, the most succulent of shellfish.

2 or 3 prawns per person, depending on size
25 g (1 oz) butter
1 tbsp olive oil

To garnish
some unblemished sorrel leaves
a little chopped parsley

For the mayonnaise
1 handful fresh sorrel
3 egg yolks
300 ml (½ pint) good quality olive oil
1–2 tbsp lemon juice
salt and pepper

1. Chop the sorrel, removing any tough stems. Pour boiling water over and leave to stand for 10 minutes, then strain and liquidize to a purée.
2. Make the mayonnaise (see p. 20) and stir in the puréed sorrel.
3. Leave the prawns in their shells, rinse well under cold running water and pat dry with kitchen paper. In a large frying pan heat the olive oil and butter. (The oil will stop the butter from burning.) Fry the prawns briskly for 4 minutes, turning from time to time.

4. Serve the prawns straight from the pan, garnished with a whole sorrel leaf and a little chopped parsley, and hand the sorrel mayonnaise separately.

M   Not suitable for microwave cookery

F   Not suitable for freezing; the mayonnaise will separate

AP Prepare the mayonnaise in advance, cook the prawns at time of serving

Mussel broth
Cawl cregyn gleision

With three quarters of Wales surrounded by sea coast it is not surprising that the Welsh are spoilt for choice when it comes to fish. Recently on the south coast new mussel beds have been established, but it is on the north coast, particularly around the island of Anglesey, that mussels are found in abundance. In fact a commercial business now gathers, cleans, prepares and delivers mussels all over North Wales and to the large markets. Enterprising, these North Walians!

900 g (2 lb) fresh mussels in
    their shells
1 medium onion, chopped
2 cloves garlic, crushed with
    salt
12 g (½ oz) butter
75 g (3 oz) fresh white
    breadcrumbs

1 tbsp lemon juice
100 ml (4 fl oz) dry white
    wine
4 tbsp cream, single or double
2 tbsp parsley, chopped

1. Scrub the mussels thoroughly and cover completely with cold water in a large pan. Bring to the boil and cook until the shells open – approximately 3 minutes.
2. Strain the liquor off the mussels and boil it hard to reduce it to 900 ml (1½ pints).
3. Meanwhile, remove the top shells and the little weed or 'beard' from the mussels, discarding any mussels that are stubborn to open.
4. In a separate saucepan cook the onion and garlic gently in the butter. Pour on the reduced mussel juice and add the breadcrumbs, lemon juice and wine. Bring to the boil and return the mussels to the soup to reheat.

5. Add the cream and the parsley but don't let the soup boil or the cream will curdle.
6. Ladle the mussels into soup bowls, pour over the broth and serve immediately.

● This makes a good meal in itself, and I suggest that you put a basket of hot crusty bread and some butter on the table to complete the meal.

M   Suitable for microwave cookery

F   Freeze at the end of stage 4. Add the cream and parsley after reheating

AP Prepare up to the end of stage 4

Marinated salmon with honey and mustard sauce

Eog mel a mwstard

Salmon fishing on the south-western peninsula of Wales (Dyfed) has for centuries been distinguished by the use of coracles and nets. The coracle is a light, manoeuvrable craft, 'a swimmer of animal skin' as one medieval bard described it. It was originally made of animal hide stretched over a framework of willow osiers, but now tar-coated canvas is used.

350 g (12 oz) fillet of
   extremely fresh salmon
   (wild Welsh salmon if
   possible)
2 tsp salt
2 tsp caster sugar
1 tbsp fresh dill, chopped, or
   1 tsp dried dill
freshly ground white pepper
1 tsp grated lemon rind

For the sauce
3 tbsp olive oil
1 tsp French mustard
1 tsp honey
1 tbsp lemon juice
seasoning to taste

To garnish
sprigs of fresh dill
slices of lemon

1. First prepare the salmon by removing any bones still left in the fillet with tweezers.
2. Lay it down the centre of a piece of clingfilm and scatter the salt, sugar, dill, pepper and lemon rind evenly over the top. Wrap tightly in the clingfilm and leave in the fridge to marinate for 24 hours.
3. For the sauce, simply combine all the ingredients in a screw-top jar and shake vigorously until well blended.
4. Serve the salmon, at room temperature, in thin slices cut down through the fillet and garnished with sprigs of fresh dill and slices of lemon. Pass the sauce separately.

- Thinly sliced brown bread and butter or a hot herb loaf would be good accompaniments.

M –

F Freeze marinated salmon in slices; thaw in fridge overnight. The sauce can be frozen if necessary, but will keep well in the fridge for a couple of weeks

AP Marinate the salmon and prepare the sauce 24 hours in advance. Serve at room temperature

Chilled salmon and leek soup
Cawl oer o eog a chennin

Teifi salmon has such a fine flavour that I suggest you seek some out. If, however, West Wales is out of reach then use any fresh salmon available, but remember the finer the flavour the better the soup.

1.2 l (2 pints) water
100 ml (4 fl oz) dry white wine
salt and freshly ground black pepper
1 bay leaf
225 g (8 oz) fresh salmon – a tailpiece would be perfect
12 g (½ oz) butter
1 stick celery, chopped

1 medium onion, chopped
175 g (6 oz) leeks, white part only, chopped
100 g (4 oz) potatoes, peeled and diced
300 ml (10 fl oz) double cream

To garnish
chopped chives

1. First prepare a *court bouillon* in which to cook the salmon: in a large saucepan bring the water to the boil, then add the wine, seasonings and bay leaf and lower the salmon in.
2. Simmer the fish very gently so that the water hardly bubbles, for 10 minutes. Remove from heat and cool in the cooking juices. Then lift the salmon carefully out of the water and flake the flesh off the bone. Strain the liquid.
3. In a fresh saucepan melt the butter and cook the celery, onion and leeks over a low heat until soft. Add the potatoes and salmon stock and simmer for 45 minutes.
4. Cool, liquidize until smooth, then chill for at least 2 hours.
5. To serve: combine the chilled mixture and the flaked salmon, add the cream and extra seasoning if necessary. Sprinkle chopped chives over the finished soup.

M   Will adapt to microwave cooking but I think it would cause more trouble than it's worth

F   Will freeze, but add cream after thawing

AP Prepare the soup up to the end of stage 4

Welsh bouillabaisse
Bouillabaisse Cymreig

This may be a contradiction in culinary terms, for a fisherman in Provence would not consider it possible to make bouillabaisse anywhere but on the shores of the Mediterranean. It is true that some varieties of fish are not available to us in our cold water climes but nevertheless we can produce a real party piece with this Welsh bouillabaisse which ideally combines at least a dozen fresh fish. Ask your fishmonger to throw in some fish heads and the odd crab claw or cockle (like mine does).

900 g (2 lb) mixed fresh fish, cleaned and gutted – as many varieties as possible: halibut, plaice, dabs, hake, skate, turbot, brill, mackerel, mullet, herring and any shellfish available, particularly a small crab
1.5 l (2½ pints) water
4 cloves garlic, crushed with salt
1 handful parsley, chopped
1 sprig fennel, chopped
1 tbsp fresh sage or marjoram, chopped
1 bay leaf
1 small onion, chopped

good pinch saffron – strands or powder
2 tbsp olive oil
1 tomato, peeled (see p. 21) and chopped
1 small red chilli, deseeded and cut into fine strips
3 potatoes, peeled and diced
salt and freshly ground black pepper
50 ml (2 fl oz) white wine
4 slices one-day-old French bread

To garnish
chopped parsley or wild garlic leaves

1. Prepare the fish first: cut the flesh from the bones and reserve, then put all the fish heads, tails and bones in a large

saucepan with the water. Add the garlic, herbs, onion and saffron and simmer for 30 minutes. Strain.

2. In a large, heavy-based saucepan heat the olive oil. Add the tomato, chilli and potato, cook gently for 2 minutes, then pour in the strained fish stock. Cut the fish flesh into chunks and add to the soup with wine and seasoning. Simmer for about 20 minutes until the potatoes are soft and the fish cooked.

3. Put the slices of bread in the bottom of a large tureen, pour the bouillabaisse over and garnish with finely chopped parsley or wild garlic leaves.

M   Not suitable for microwave cookery

F   Freeze the soup at the end of stage 2. Thaw completely before reheating very gently to stop the fish from disintegrating

AP Prepare the recipe up to the end of stage 2

Anglesey eggs
Wyau mon

A fine combination of eggs in a cheese sauce surrounded by creamy potatoes and leeks, and grilled until crisp on top. What better way to start a meal?

450 g (1 lb) potatoes, peeled
3 leeks, chopped
50 g (2 oz) butter
50 g (2 oz) flour
600 ml (1 pint) milk

75 g (3 oz) Caerphilly cheese, grated
salt and freshly ground pepper
4 eggs, hardboiled and shelled

1. Boil the potatoes in salted water until soft. Cook the leeks in salted water for 10 minutes, or add to the potatoes for the last 10 minutes of their cooking time. Drain well then combine, season and mash together.
2. Make a cheese sauce by melting the butter in a saucepan, stir in the flour and cook for a minute, then gradually stir in the milk and bring to the boil to thicken. Season well and add half of the cheese.
3. Take 4 individual dishes – ramekins or scallop shells are ideal – and with a fork arrange the leek and potato mixture around the sides. Chop the eggs and put in the middle of each dish. Cover with the cheese sauce and sprinkle over the remaining cheese.
4. Brown quickly under a hot grill or heat through in a very hot oven (gas 8, 450°F, 230°C) for 10 minutes. Serve at once.

M   Not suitable for microwave cookery

F   Not suitable – the eggs will turn rubbery

AP Prepare up to the end of stage 3

Grapefruit with mead
Grawnffrwyth gyda medd

'Bees derive their noble descent from Paradise: when owing to man's transgression, they were thence expelled, God gave them his blessing; on this account Mass cannot properly be sung without their wax.' So wrote Hywel Dda when he codified the existing laws of Wales in the 10th century. Even the bees came under his scrutiny, or maybe it was the recognition of mead as an alcoholic beverage.

This is a simple but successful way to serve grapefruit and a light, appetizing dish to serve before a filling main course.

2 large grapefruit, pink-fleshed ones if possible
1 tsp fresh ginger, grated

4 tbsp mead (dry sherry with a little honey would substitute)

To garnish
4 sugared mint leaves

1. Cut the grapefruit in half horizontally, then cut round the edges to loosen the segments. Pick out any pips.
2. Sprinkle over the ginger and spoon over the mead.
3. Flash the grapefruit under a very hot grill for 2 minutes to heat through and set off the delicate aroma of the mead and ginger.
4. Serve at once garnished with sugared mint leaves.
- To sugar a mint leaf, just brush it with egg white and dip in caster sugar so that it collects an even covering.

M Not suitable for microwave cookery

F Not suitable for freezing

AP Prepare up to the end of stage 2

Deep-fried cockles
Cocos wedi'u ffrio

The collecting of cockles on the sands of South Wales has changed little over the past fifty years. Not an enviable job for the women who return to the sands every day except Sunday whatever the weather, summer and winter. They use a sickle-shaped iron 'scrape' to break up the sand, and then rake the cockles into piles. Even today, no mechanical vehicles such as tractors are permitted on the sands. The only change is that ponies have replaced many of the donkeys that accompany the women, carrying the full sacks of cockles for the return journey.

450 g (1 lb) fresh cooked
   cockles

For the batter
150 ml (¼ pint) water
1 tbsp sunflower or safflower
   oil
100 g (4 oz) flour
pinch of salt
1 egg white

To serve
freshly ground black pepper

For the mayonnaise sauce
4 tbsp homemade (see p. 20)
   or good-quality bought
   mayonnaise mixed with 1 of
   the following:
grated rind and juice of ½
   lemon
1 clove garlic, crushed with
   salt
1 tbsp walnuts, very finely
   chopped

1. Prepare the batter by pouring the water and oil into a liquidizer. Add the flour and salt and blend until smooth. Let the batter stand for an hour.
2. Just before cooking, whisk the egg white to soft peaks and fold into the batter.

3. Dip the cockles into the batter and fry a few at a time in hot oil. Drain on absorbent kitchen paper.
4. Serve immediately with either garlic-, walnut- or lemon-flavoured mayonnaise and lots of freshly ground black pepper.

M   Not suitable for microwave cookery

F   Not suitable for freezing

AP Prepare up to end of stage 1

Crab and laver parcels
Parseli cranc a bara lawr

Catching crabs off the Pembroke coast has long been sport for young and old alike. There is an annual competition off the harbour wall at Newport, Pembroke, where as many as fifty little crabs are pulled from the water on the end of a string to which has been attached a juicy limpet. These tiny crabs are quickly returned to the sea but their larger brothers and sisters, pulled from the deeper waters by fishermen, usually end up on the dining table. Crabmeat is now available fresh or frozen, and for this dish I suggest that you use a combination of white and brown meat to give a richer filling.

If your guests need some persuasion to try laverbread just remind them that Richard Burton used to call it 'the Welshman's caviar'!

100 g (4 oz) crabmeat
50 g (2 oz) mushrooms, chopped
50 g (2 oz) laverbread (or substitute 50 g (2 oz) spinach, cooked and chopped)
100 g (4 oz) curd cheese
2 spring onions or a handful of chives, chopped

freshly ground black pepper
a little beaten egg (optional)
225 g (8 oz) filo pastry
melted butter

To garnish
lettuce leaves
fresh herbs

1. Using a fork, combine the crabmeat, mushrooms, laverbread, curd cheese, spring onions and pepper. Add some beaten egg if the mixture is too dry to hold together.
2. Divide the sheets of filo pastry into two piles. With a sharp pair of kitchen scissors cut through them lengthways at 4 cm

(1½ in) intervals, so that you have four long strips of filo pastry with each stack of sheets. Brush the top layer of the filo strips with melted butter.

3. Divide the crab filling into eight and put one portion at the end of each strip of pastry. Fold the pastry by bringing one corner over the filling and across to the side to form a triangle. Fold again to maintain the triangle shape and continue to fold until the whole pastry strip has been used up.

4. Brush the parcels with melted butter and bake in a hot oven (gas 7, 425°F, 220°C) for 10–15 minutes until crisp and golden brown.

5. Serve the parcels warm or cold with a garnish of lettuce and fresh herbs.

M   Not suitable for microwave cookery

F   Freeze cooked crab parcels. Reheat from frozen

AP Prepare to the end of stage 3

Laverbread cakes with bacon
Bara lawr

Laverbread is still very much part of the Welsh diet. Collected mainly by hand on the Pembrokeshire and Gower coast, the laver is boiled for about 5 hours in small factories situated right beside the sea before finding its way to local markets and fishmongers. Should you collect your own laver from the Welsh coastline wash it well under fresh running water and simmer until soft and well pulped, but don't allow all the texture to disintegrate with overcooking. Laverbread is eaten as a breakfast delicacy, with added oatmeal to thicken the consistency and lots of black pepper to season. Bacon is traditionally served with laverbread, and the fat gives a particularly good flavour for cooking.

450 g (1 lb) prepared
   laverbread
lots of freshly ground black
   pepper

50 g (2 oz) oatmeal
4 rashers smoked bacon
4 slices of bread

1. Divide the laverbread into four portions, season well with the black pepper and coat with the oatmeal.
2. Fry the bacon in its own fat and remove from pan when crisp.
3. Add the laverbread cakes to the bacon fat in the pan and fry over medium heat for 5 minutes, turning once.
4. Toast the bread and serve the laverbread cakes on top garnished with the rashers of bacon.
- Laverbread cakes can also be made from mashed potato combined with cooked laverbread in a mixture of 2 parts potato to 1 part laver. Add a little grated onion, a raw egg and lots of seasoning. Shape and cook as above. Eat for

breakfast with a fry-up, with any lamb dish, or with a sour cream and chive sauce.

M   Suitable for microwave cookery

F   Freeze uncooked

AP Prepare up to the end of stage 1

Leek and potato soup
Cawl cennin a thatws

This traditional Welsh soup, warm and filling on a cold winter's day, can be transformed into a sophisticated chilled vichyssoise for those balmy summer evenings.

1 rasher bacon, diced
25 g (1 oz) butter
2 large leeks, chopped
450 g (1 lb) potatoes, peeled and diced
900 ml (1½ pints) chicken stock
300 ml (½ pint) milk

2 tbsp parsley, chopped
salt and freshly ground black pepper
lemon juice to taste (optional)

To garnish
cream
chopped parsley

1. In a large saucepan fry the diced bacon in the butter. Add the leeks and potatoes and cook gently for 5 minutes.
2. Pour in the stock and milk, bring to the boil, then simmer for 20 minutes.
3. Cool slightly then liquidize and season to taste, adding a squeeze of lemon juice if the flavour is too bland.
4. To serve, pour the soup into bowls, swirl a spoonful of cream into each one and add a sprinkling of parsley.

- As a main meal soup, serve unblended so the pieces of bacon and vegetable are left intact, with perhaps a bowl of grated Cheddar cheese or even some slices of frankfurter sausage added.
- For an iced summer soup, try adding a dash of cold white wine.

M Suitable for microwave cookery

F Freezes well

AP Prepare the soup up to the end of stage 3. Reheat to serve

Sorrel parcels with yogurt cheese and prawns

Parseli suran gyda chorgimychiaid

This is a classic combination of Welsh fare. Sorrel, which flourishes throughout Wales, yogurt, now produced by a large proportion of dairy farmers, and prawns plucked from our extensive coastline. Making a soft cheese out of yogurt is most satisfying and the texture is creamy, but I find that low-fat natural yogurt makes too sharp a cheese for most people's taste. The Greek-style yogurt, on the other hand, produces a softer flavour which you may prefer. Lettuce leaves can be substituted for the sorrel.

450 g (1 lb) Greek-style yogurt
    or plain natural yogurt
8 large sorrel leaves
100 g (4 oz) prawns, cooked
    and peeled

2–3 tbsp mayonnaise
cayenne pepper to taste

To garnish
8 prawns

1. First prepare a soft cheese from the yogurt. To do this you simply need to drain the yogurt of most of its liquid contents. I find a coffee filter paper works well, but you could pour the yogurt into a sieve lined with a clean 'J' cloth. Leave to drip overnight in a cool place and by the morning you will have a well-flavoured soft cheese.
2. Blanch the sorrel by plunging the leaves into boiling water for 8–10 seconds, then rinse under the cold tap to cool quickly so that they retain their green colour.
3. Mix the yogurt, prawns, mayonnaise and cayenne pepper and divide between the eight sorrel leaves. Fold the leaves over the filling to make into parcels and garnish with a prawn on top of each.

- Serve with some brown rolls or brown bread and butter to offset the richness of this delicious dish.

M –

F Not suitable for freezing

AP Make up to 3 hours in advance and chill in fridge. To restore gloss on sorrel leaves brush with olive oil just before serving

Granny Griffiths' cawl
Cawl nain Griffiths

Ask any Welsh housewife for her cawl recipe and it will without a doubt differ from that of her neighbours. Recipes for cawl are legion, and I am including this one to demonstrate just how flexible a recipe can be! There are regional differences, with some Welsh cooks using pork and others swearing by lamb as the main ingredient. Oatmeal, flour or potatoes can be used to thicken cawl, but one thing is universal – leeks are a vital ingredient. They must only be added at the very end of cooking to preserve their texture and colour. Recently a friend told me that her Granny always sprinkled marigold petals over the steaming bowls of cawl. She thought it was to tempt the children to eat up but I think that it was more of a traditional decoration.

This is a friend's family recipe and I reproduce it here exactly as it came to me.

You will need a piece of lamb, beef or ham, suitable for slicing when cooked. Place in a saucepan – or cauldron if you have one – cover with water, bring slowly to simmering point and cook till tender. This will take approximately 20 minutes per lb.

Meanwhile prepare carrots, potatoes, swedes, parsnips, onions, cutting them into pieces to your liking. When the meat is cooked remove it from the liquid and set aside. Put all the vegetables into the meat stock and *simmer* till tender, adding salt, pepper and a good sprig of savory. When vegetables are cooked replace meat and add a finely shredded leek, including the green part, and some chopped parsley. The cawl must not boil at this point but simmer gently for about 3–4 minutes. Remove the meat and place on a dish. If a thicker stock is required mix a tablespoonful of fine oatmeal with a little water and add while the vegetables are cooking. The meat should be sliced and served with the cawl. It is very good eaten cold the next day.

No quantities are given in this recipe. The amount of meat and vegetables depends on numbers to be fed and the size of their appetites. Traditionally cawl is eaten with a wooden spoon out of small wooden bowls, and it is not uncommon for dumplings to find their way into this all-inclusive meal! For a more conventional cawl recipe see page 60.

Green pancakes
Crempogau gwyrdd

I first ate these delicious and wholesome-looking pancakes at the Lake Hotel in Llangammarch Wells, the very heart of Wales. Most of the vegetables are grown within the hotel grounds and this recipe was made entirely from locally produced foods.

For the batter
1 egg
25 g (1 oz) melted butter
1 tbsp cooked spinach, chopped (frozen works well)
salt and freshly ground black pepper
300 ml (½ pt) milk
75 g (3 oz) white flour
25 g (1 oz) wholemeal flour
olive oil for frying

For the filling
450 g (1 lb) fresh broccoli
175–225 g (6–8 oz) Pencarreg Welsh farmhouse cheese (or substitute Brie)

To garnish
fresh herbs, finely chopped

1. In a blender mix the egg, butter, spinach and seasoning. Add the milk and flour and blend to a smooth batter.
2. Steam the broccoli or boil in a minimum of water until cooked but still crisp.
3. In a 20 cm (8 in) frying pan cook at least 8 pancakes (see p. 21).
4. Place a piece of broccoli and a slice of Pencarreg on each pancake, roll up, and place on a baking tray. Cover with foil and heat in a moderate oven (gas 4, 350°F, 180°C) for about 20 minutes or until the cheese has melted.
5. Garnish with finely chopped fresh herbs and serve on their own or with a sour cream sauce.

- *Sour cream sauce* Mix a 150 ml (5 fl oz) pot of sour cream with a crushed clove of garlic, some finely chopped chives and a good grind of black pepper.

M   Stages 2 and 4 can be performed in a microwave

F   Can be frozen but the crisp texture of the broccoli may be lost. Reheat from frozen in a warm oven or microwave

AP Prepare the pancakes up to the end of stage 4

Ceredigion cawl

This is the recipe used by the natives of Ceredigion, a region on the west coast of Wales. Ceredigion's fifty-two-mile coastline looks out over Cardigan Bay, and the natives of Ceredigion are known as the 'Cardis'. They guard their heritage well, many still speaking Welsh as their first language. Visitors to this beautiful part of Wales are, as ever, guaranteed a fine welcome with, more than likely, a bowl of warming cawl served with a wooden spoon.

This recipe should be prepared and cooked over 2 days.

Serves 6–8 as both a soup and a main course

1 k (2 lb) bacon hock
1 k (2 lb) shin of beef
225 g (8 oz) carrots, sliced
225 g (8 oz) swedes, peeled
and diced
450 g (1 lb) potatoes, peeled
and quartered
2 parsnips, sliced

2 medium onions, 1 left whole
and 1 peeled and sliced
2 leeks, sliced
25 g (1 oz) fresh parsley,
chopped
2 tbsp porridge oats
freshly ground black pepper
to taste

1. Day 1. Soak the hock in cold water for 1 hour. Drain, then put in a large saucepan with the beef and the whole onion. Cover with water and bring to the boil. Simmer gently for 2 hours then leave to cool overnight.
2. Day 2. Skim off fat from the surface of the meat. Bring to the boil and add the swede and carrot. Simmer for 15 minutes.
3. Add the potatoes, parsnip and onion, simmer until cooked, about 20 minutes. Add the leeks, parsley and oats. Boil for a few minutes.
4. To serve, remove meat from the cawl. Ladle the soup into a

large tureen or individual soup bowls. Serve with chunks of fresh bread. As a main course, slice the meat and eat either with vegetables from the cawl or some freshly prepared vegetables.

- The meat may be kept for another day and eaten cold or diced and added into the soup again.

M   Suitable for microwave cookery

F   Suitable for freezing as long as the cawl isn't too salty. It will keep for a few days in the fridge, just reheat to boiling each day

AP   Make up the soup recipe entirely, reheat when required

Marinated herrings with apple and lemon yogurt

Penwaig gydag afal a iogwrt lemwn

Fresh herrings were sold from barrows in Fishguard not so long ago, and these inexpensive fish were a major part of the fishing industry on the west coast. Eaten fresh or salted away for the winter the herring was a regular feature in the diets of coast-dwelling Welsh families. In this recipe the sharpness of the apple and lemon yogurt cuts into the oily flesh of the herrings and together they blend to give a good clean flavour.

2–3 good-sized, very fresh
  herrings, filleted
salt and freshly ground black
  pepper
grated rind and juice of 1
  lemon
3 tbsp olive oil
3–4 tbsp white wine vinegar
1 tbsp honey

200 ml (7 fl oz) plain yogurt
1 small onion, finely sliced
2 red-skinned apples, diced
2 bay leaves
1 tbsp fresh dill, chopped

To garnish
fresh dill
red-skinned apple

1. Cut the fish into 2.5 cm (1 in) chunks. Season very well with salt and pepper.
2. Combine the lemon rind, juice, oil, vinegar and honey with the yogurt, then stir in the onion, apple, bay leaves and dill.
3. Fold in the herring chunks and leave to marinate for at least 24 hours in the fridge.
4. Serve on individual plates or in tall stemmed glasses, garnished with dill and slices of red-skinned apple.
• Pumpernickel, the German rye bread, makes a good accompaniment.

M –

F Not suitable; the sauce will separate

AP Prepare up to the end of stage 3

Parsley pie
Pastai persli

Parsley pie used to be eaten cold for afternoon tea on the Gower Peninsula earlier this century. This and many other insights into Wales's past were given to me by Mrs Minwel Tibbott, who is Assistant Keeper in the Department of Buildings and Domestic Life at the Welsh Folk Museum, St Fagans, in South Glamorgan. She has compiled and written an authoritative book on traditional dishes entitled *Welsh Fare*.

Nothing has changed much, for savoury pies are still the perfect answer for a busy family with flexible mealtimes. Eaten hot, warm or cold an egg flan never ruins.

For the pastry
75 g (3 oz) butter or firm
   margarine
175 g (6 oz) plain flour
pinch of salt
a little cold water to mix

To garnish
sliced tomato

For the filling
1 egg and 1 yolk
50 g (2 oz) Caerphilly cheese,
   grated
150 ml (¼ pint) milk
6 spring onions, finely
   chopped
1 tbsp fresh parsley, chopped
salt and freshly ground black
   pepper

1. Make up the pastry by rubbing the butter into the flour until it resembles fine breadcrumbs. Stir in the salt and add just enough cold water to make a firm dough. Knead lightly until well blended then chill for 30 minutes.
2. Meanwhile, make the filling: in a bowl combine the egg, egg yolk, cheese, milk, onions, parsley and seasoning. Stir well.
3. Roll out the pastry and line an 18 cm (7 in) flan case or shallow pie dish. Pour in the filling and bake the pie in a

moderately hot oven (gas 6, 400°F, 200°C) for about 30 minutes, until firm and golden brown.

4. For maximum flavour, serve warm, with a garnish of sliced tomato.

M Suitable for microwave cookery

F For best results freeze the filled pie uncooked. Cook direct from frozen

AP Prepare and cook the flan in advance. Keep in fridge overnight or until needed then reheat in a very slow oven (gas ½, 250°F, 130°C) for 15 minutes or just sit the flan in a warm corner of the kitchen

Fried goat's cheese with rhubarb sauce
Caws gafr wedi'i ffrio gyda saws riwbob

Abergavenny in Gwent was at one time the 'goat centre' of Wales. Although keeping goats has not been popular recently, goat's milk was the preferred milk for making cheese throughout Britain up until the end of the 18th century. It differs from cow's milk in its composition, fat content and structure, making a fine-textured, creamy cheese with a tangy flavour. Goat's cheese, both soft and hard, and goat's milk are readily available throughout Wales and if you want to process your own soft cheese there is even a Welsh dried goat's milk on the market too. Tony Craske who makes a variety of soft goat's cheeses on his farm in Mamilhad, Gwent recommends this recipe for fried goat's cheese. It is quite delicious but rather rich, so he suggests you prepare a sharp fruit sauce to serve with it.

225 g (8 oz) soft goat's cheese
flour, seasoned with salt,
   pepper and a little dried
   thyme
1 egg, beaten with a little milk
fresh breadcrumbs for coating
1 tbsp oil
25 g (1 oz) butter

For the rhubarb sauce
225 g (8 oz) rhubarb
grated rind and juice of 1
   orange
sugar to taste
½ tsp powdered ginger
   (optional)
4 slices wholemeal bread cut
   into discs and toasted

1. Divide the goat's cheese into 4, shape into flattish discs and roll in the seasoned flour.
2. Brush the cheese discs with the beaten egg then toss them in the breadcrumbs, patting the crumbs on with a knife if necessary. Repeat this stage so that each cheese has a really

good covering of egg and breadcrumbs. Chill the cheeses in the fridge for half an hour.

3. Make up the sauce: trim the rhubarb, cut into chunks and stew in a very little water with the orange juice and grated rind. (Use a non-metallic container if possible, such as a Pyrex casserole, to avoid upsetting the acidity in the rhubarb.) Sweeten to taste, add the ginger and allow to cool.

4. To fry the cheeses, heat the oil and butter in a frying pan and when it sizzles, carefully add the cheeses. Cook for 3–4 minutes on each side, turning only once to avoid them breaking. Alternatively, deep fry in hot oil.

5. Serve the cheeses straight from the pan, sitting on the toasted discs of wholemeal bread, with the sauce passed separately.

M The sauce could be prepared in the microwave

F Freeze only the sauce

AP Prepare up to the end of stage 3

FISH

Gower cockle and bacon pie
Scallops with samphire
Salmon with Teifi sauce
Watercress-filled trout
Tenby dabs
Mussels with parsley and tomato sauce
Stuffed herrings
Hake with fennel sauce
Skate with sorrel sauce
Sewin with Pembroke sauce
Bard's fish dish
Devilled crab
Cockles and pasta
Aberaeron mackerel
Trout cooked in leeks
Mackerel with oranges
Roulade of fresh salmon, with an avocado
   and smoked salmon filling
Sea bass with garlic sauce
Scallops in gin
Fisherman's pie
Laverbread, mussel and tomato tart

Not only is Wales surrounded by the sea on three sides, but inland we have lakes galore, and a fine collection of clear, fast-flowing rivers, so a good selection of fresh fish is guaranteed.

Cockles, a passion with the Welsh, are as popular now as they have always been over the centuries. Eaten fresh from the sea with a dusting of pepper and a dab of vinegar they are delicious. Collecting cockles is a back-breaking job and the rewards were mean for the colliers' wives who used to collect them in Pembroke. If the tedious task of scratching for cockles in the sand wasn't bad enough, then the long journey on foot to Carmarthen market to sell their pickings must have made the job a real test of courage and strength for the hard-working Welsh women.

Crabs flourish off the craggy rocks around the Welsh coast-line, and visitors will be offered fresh crab in most seaside cafés and restaurants. With its rich flavour and mixture of dark and white meats crab is still a luxury sold at a reasonable price. Lobsters have suffered from being overfished in recent years but are now being reseeded in the Menai Straights to replenish the depleted stocks. Mussels abound on the northern shores, especially around Anglesey, and oysters are being reseeded in Pembroke Dock on the south coast. Queen scallops, members of the scallop family, are found in the waters all round the south-western peninsula, so much so that they tear the nets of the trawlers. All these shellfish can be found for sale along the Welsh coasts or inland where they are sold from vans on a weekly basis.

Sewin, the Welsh name for the sea trout, is a member of the brown trout family which escapes to the sea only to return to Welsh rivers, in particular to the fast-flowing Teifi, Towy and

Cleddau in Dyfed. A delicious, delicate pink fish, it is preferred by many to the fine salmon also found in Welsh rivers. Luckily sewin are for sale on the marble slabs of local fishmongers throughout Wales, and their freshness is guaranteed.

Alas, many of the fish which are gathered on and off the Welsh coastline go directly to the large markets of Liverpool in the north and Milford Haven in the south. From here they are transported to Billingsgate fish market in London where a percentage will then travel back to Wales. Milford Haven dock is undergoing redevelopment at the moment and it is hoped that vessels suitable for operating in the exposed, offshore deep waters will bring in a greater selection of fish. Skateray makes the greatest part of the catch at the moment with hake, plaice and cod coming next. Ask the fishermen why they don't sell their catch locally and they say that the demand is regular and the price better in London. But change is in the air, for restaurateurs know what they want in the way of fish and they also know what is available. So once contacts have been made with local fishermen and good prices, comparable with London ones, are agreed, fresher-than-fresh local specialities find their way on to the menus.

Fish is, of course, good for us, being very low in fat and easily digestible. Quickly cooked and not needing much in the way of added flavours or sauces, it should be on our plates at least twice a week. Microwave ovens cook fish well, in a minimum of time, with very little or no extra fat and with little bother. Some small fish such as river trout have very delicate flavours and to enjoy them at their best I suggest that you remove the backbone before cooking (see p. 18) so that you can eat them without the distraction of a mouthful of spiky bones.

When shopping for fish always make sure that they are absolutely fresh. Look for fish with firm, even-textured flesh, clear, full and shiny eyes, bright red gills and a clean sea smell. Steaks, cutlets and fillets should have firm, closely packed flakes; any with a fibrous or watery appearance are stale. Fish whose flesh has a blue or green tinge is probably none too fresh; check both sides of the fish before you buy it. The very

best way to buy fish is to get to know your fishmonger and
return to him regularly, asking his advice on the choice of fish.
He will, more often than not, have some good recipes for the
more unusual species too.

Gower cockle and bacon pie
Pastai gwyr

Cockles were popular with the Romans in Wales. Excavated sites have revealed vast quantities of their shells. They have remained a common food for coastal dwellers throughout the centuries and cooked fresh cockles are still sold from vans and market stalls throughout South Wales. Collected from Penclawdd on the Gower peninsula, the 'cockle women' retreat before the incoming tide with heavy baskets of shellfish, which are then boiled in the village co-operative factory.

450 g (1 lb) smoked bacon, cut into fine strips
1 large onion, chopped
50 g (2 oz) butter
50 g (2 oz) flour
600 ml (1 pint) milk
450 g (1 lb) fresh, cooked cockles
1 handful chives, chopped
100 ml (4 fl oz) dry white wine

salt and freshly ground black pepper

For the pie topping
450 g (1 lb) potatoes, boiled
1 small leek, finely grated
25 g (1 oz) butter, melted
salt and freshly ground black pepper
50 g (2 oz) Cheddar cheese, grated

1. In a medium-sized saucepan, gently fry the bacon strips and onion in the butter for 5 minutes. Stir in the flour and cook for another 2 minutes without browning.
2. Gradually add the milk, stirring continuously, bring to the boil and add the cockles, chives, wine and seasoning. Bring back to the boil and simmer for 10 minutes. Pour into a 1.2 l (2 pint) pie dish.
3. For the topping, mash the potatoes with the leek, add the

melted butter and seasoning and spread the potato mixture over the cockles and sauce.

4. Sprinkle the grated Cheddar cheese over and bake for 30 minutes in a moderate oven (gas 4, 350°F, 180°C) until golden brown and crisp on top.

M   Suitable for microwave cookery. Brown under a grill if necessary to finish

F   A good dish to freeze. Reheat from frozen

AP Prepare up to the end of stage 3

Scallops with samphire
Cregyn cylchog gyda chorn carw'r mor

Scallops are in season from October to March and, like all shellfish, should be bought alive. The small Queen scallops found around the coast of Wales are worth seeking out; make friends with a fisherman to guarantee your supply. Handle with care as the flesh of scallops is very delicate, especially the bright orange coral or roe, and overcooking will make the flesh rubbery.

If scallops, samphire and sorrel are all unavailable, then substitute prawns, beanshoots and spinach. This mixture will give you the same delicious crunchy texture but taste carefully and add lemon juice if necessary.

225 g (8 oz) fresh samphire
  (or substitute bean shoots)
8 good-sized scallops (12–16 if
  small Queen scallops)
50 g (2 oz) butter
3 sorrel leaves, roughly
  chopped (or substitute 3
  spinach leaves)

1 tbsp dry white wine
freshly ground black pepper

To garnish
wild garlic leaves, chopped
  (or substitute parsley)

1. Pick over the samphire and blanch it by tossing it into boiling water for a minute then rinsing well under the cold tap.
2. Clean the scallops and carefully detach the coral. Reserve any juices. Cut each scallop into 3 pieces.
3. Melt the butter in a large frying pan and fry the scallop pieces gently for 3 minutes. Add the corals and cook for another minute.
4. Toss in the samphire, sorrel, wine and reserved scallop juices, and season well with black pepper. Cook for 1

minute, stirring well, then serve immediately with a sprinkling of freshly chopped wild garlic leaves.

● This dish is rich and should be served with a plainish
vegetable accompaniment. A purée of potatoes, perhaps, or
some plain boiled rice flavoured with fresh herbs.

M This dish is microwaveable, but easier to control over
conventional heat

F Not suitable for freezing

AP Prepare the scallops and samphire in advance but cook at
the last minute

Salmon with Teifi sauce
Eog gyda saws Teifi

'The noble river Teivi (Teifi) flows here, and abounds with the finest salmon, more than any other river in Wales,' said Giraldus Cambrensis (Gerald the Welshman), writing towards the end of the 12th century.

In her cookbook of 1867 Lady Llanover gives a recipe for Teifi sauce and I have taken her basic ingredients but modified them a little. '¾ pint melted butter with a glass of port' seems more than a modern stomach needs!

4 salmon steaks
1 tbsp fresh herbs or 1 tsp
   dried

For the sauce
25 g (1 oz) butter
1 medium onion, finely
   chopped

1 anchovy fillet, soaked in
   milk for 10 minutes
1 tsp tomato purée
50 ml (2 fl oz) port (substitute
   sherry if necessary)
salt and freshly ground black
   pepper
150 ml (5 fl oz) plain yogurt

1. Lay each salmon steak on a piece of well-buttered grease-proof paper or foil. Season well with salt and pepper and lay some fresh herbs on top. Make parcels out of the greaseproof paper or foil by bringing the edges together and twisting to seal.
2. Cook the salmon parcels on a baking tray in a moderate oven (gas 4, 350°F, 180°C) for 15 minutes. Leave unopened until ready to serve.
3. For the sauce, melt the butter in a saucepan and cook the onion very gently for five minutes. Add the anchovy fillet cut into small pieces, the tomato purée, port and seasoning and boil up well.

4. Take the pan off the heat, stir in the yogurt and serve the
   sauce at once with the salmon parcels. Either take the salmon
   steaks out of the wrappers before you serve them or alternatively present each guest with an unopened parcel.

M   Suitable for microwave cookery (don't use foil)

F   Not suitable for freezing

AP Prepare up to the end of stage 1. Cook the sauce but add
    the yogurt when reheating

Watercress-filled trout

Brithyll gyda berw'r dŵr

'My father taught me to tickle trout up on the flat rock down by Mrs Tom Jenkins.' Richard Llewellyn in *How Green Was My Valley*.

Baked trout was once a breakfast dish in Wales. On sunny summer days, quarrymen and miners used to go to their local stream and 'tickle' enough trout for breakfast.

Healthy and low-calorie, this recipe for trout gives their delicate flavour a new depth. By cooking the trout *'en papillote'* all the goodness is trapped inside the foil coat and, with a minimum of added fat, the flavour is superb.

2 bunches watercress
100 g (4 oz) curd cheese
1 tbsp creamed horseradish
1 egg, beaten
salt, freshly ground black
   pepper, grated nutmeg

4 good-sized trout, boned (see
   p. 18)

To garnish
sprigs of watercress
slices of fresh lemon

1. Reserve 4 sprigs of watercress for garnish then finely chop the rest and mix with the curd cheese, horseradish, beaten egg and seasoning.
2. Stuff the mixture into the cavities of the trout and wrap each in a large sheet of buttered foil. Put on a baking sheet and cook in a moderate oven (gas 4, 350°F, 180°C) for 20 minutes or until the flesh flakes easily.
3. Serve the trout immediately, still wrapped in the foil to allow each person the pleasure of catching those first delicious aromas as they peel open their parcel.
4. Lay the sprigs of watercress and slices of fresh lemon on the

plates alongside the foil parcels and serve with jacket potatoes and a salad.

M Suitable for microwave cookery (do not use foil)

F Not suitable for freezing

AP Prepare the filling and stuff the trout

Tenby dabs
Dabiau dinbych y pysgod

A dab is a flat fish related to plaice, but smaller with rough scales. Weighing about 225 g (8 oz) each they make a superb meal when boned and stuffed. Dabs are fished from the sea all round the British Isles, but those in Tenby are rather special, particularly when filled with prawns, capers and a knob of blue cheese. If you are daunted by the prospect of boning a dab, buy some fillets of plaice and roll them around the stuffing instead.

225 g (8 oz) shelled prawns
1 tbsp capers
100 g (4 oz) blue cheese
4 dabs, scaled and boned (see
    p. 18) – or substitute 4
    fillets of plaice

200 ml (8 fl oz) dry white
    wine
100 g (4 oz) butter

1. Combine the prawns and capers, and use to stuff the fish cavities, putting a quarter of the blue cheese in each. (Fillets of plaice should be wrapped around the filling and secured with cocktail sticks.)
2. Arrange in a shallow, ovenproof dish. Pour over half the wine and dot 25 g (1 oz) of the butter over the top. Cover with buttered foil and bake in a moderate oven (gas 4, 350°F, 180°C) for 15 minutes.
3. In a small saucepan, heat the remaining butter until it froths. Just as the butter begins to colour pour in the juices from the fish and the remaining 100 ml (4 fl oz) of wine, stirring to mix. Pour over the dabs and serve at once.
• A good partner for this dish would be plain boiled noodles to soak up the delicious juices, or some baby new Pembroke potatoes.

M   Ideal for the microwave

F   Not suitable for freezing

AP Prepare and stuff the fish

Mussels with parsley and tomato sauce
Cregyn gleision gyda phersli a thomato

Mussels are plentiful on the north coast of Wales, where they feature regularly on most restaurant menus. Many people avoid buying them because of time involved in their preparation, but a small firm called The Mytti Mussel, based on Anglesey, now cleans and washes mussels for customers and there is really no excuse to avoid these delicious shellfish any more.

I first ate this wonderful mussel dish at Ty'n Rhos Farmhouse outside Caernarfon, where Lynda Kettle cooks tirelessly for her appreciative visitors.

900 g (2 lb) fresh mussels
50 ml (2 fl oz) white wine
1 small onion, sliced
1 large stem parsley, chopped, plus 1 tbsp parsley, chopped
450 g (1 lb) fresh tomatoes, skinned (see p. 21) and chopped, or 1 large (794 g) tin

1 tbsp olive oil
1 clove garlic, crushed with salt
salt and freshly ground black pepper,
a slurp of whisky, say 25 ml (1 fl oz)

1. Unless you have a friendly fishmonger to prepare your mussels, scrub and clean them thoroughly, removing the beards and discarding any mussels with broken or open shells. Put them in a saucepan with the wine, sliced onion and parsley stem. Cover and cook over medium heat, shaking occasionally until they open.
2. Remove the mussels from their shells and set them aside. Strain the cooking liquid through a fine sieve to remove any sandy sediment and retain the wine juice.

3. Heat the oil in a large, deep frying pan and fry the garlic for a minute. Add the tomatoes, stir to break up, and toss in the 1 tbsp parsley and the seasoning. Add the reserved wine juice and simmer to reduce for 10 minutes, until the tomatoes are pulpy.

4. Stir in the mussels and whisky and taste for seasoning.

• Serve with plain boiled rice and a green salad.

M   Mussels behave beautifully in the microwave. Prepare as above but microwave them for a minimum of time, until you can see the mussels beginning to open. Continue with the whole recipe in the microwave

F   Suitable for freezing

AP   Prepare this dish up to the end of stage 3. Add the mussels just before reheating

Stuffed herrings
Penwaig wedi'i stwffio

The herring, a small round fish with oily flesh, is at its best from May to October. If you visit Wales during the summer, herrings will be offered to you in a variety of different guises – fried in oatmeal, soused, stuffed and baked, or grilled as in this recipe.

4 herrings
2 tomatoes, skinned (see
   p. 21) and chopped
2 tsp parsley, chopped
35 g (1½ oz) fresh brown
   breadcrumbs

1 small leek, chopped
salt and freshly ground black
   pepper
milk to bind

1. Clean and scale the fish, removing the roes. Open the fish and remove the backbone (see p. 18).
2. Mix together the tomatoes, parsley, breadcrumbs and chopped leek. Season well and bind the mixture with a little milk.
3. Stuff the herrings and cook uncovered in a buttered oven-proof dish in the centre of a medium oven (gas 4, 350°F, 180°C) for 30 minutes.
• The barbecue is another good way to cook the herrings: just seal the openings with cocktail sticks and grill the herrings over a charcoal grill or wood fire to which you have added a good sprig of fresh thyme. If grilling in the kitchen then place the thyme at the bottom of the grill pan to allow the aromatic flavour to penetrate the herring above.

M   Could be microwaved but don't miss out on the lovely crisp skin that oven baking or grilling affords

F   Not suitable for freezing

AP Prepare and stuff the fish

Hake with fennel sauce
Cegddu gyda saws ffenigl

This is a classic combination of Welsh food. Hake has always been the favourite white sea fish of the people of South Wales, and it was hake that started the historic fishery upon which the fish trade was founded in Milford Haven. Fennel was first introduced by the Romans and is still to be found growing wild in parts of West Wales. Being part of the anise family it will always impart a special flavour to fish. Bulb fennel, the root of the plant, is now available from many greengrocers and has a fibrous texture and subtle aniseed taste. For this dish, however, I suggest that you use the feathery herb. Good as a digestive, fennel can be replaced by a dash of pernod if you prefer, and the combination will be just as good.

4 hake steaks, about 675 g (1½ lb) in all
50 g (2 oz) butter
4 sprigs fresh fennel leaf

1 tbsp fresh parsley, finely chopped
salt and freshly ground black pepper
juice of ½ lemon

For the sauce
50 g (2 oz) butter
2 tbsp fresh fennel leaf, finely chopped

To garnish
slices of lemon
sprigs of fennel or parsley

1. Cook the hake steaks '*en papillote*' by wrapping them in some buttered tinfoil, dabbing the butter on top and adding a sprig of fresh fennel. Bake in a moderate oven (gas 4, 350°F, 180°C) for just 10 minutes or until the fish flesh is firm to the touch and has lost its translucent appearance, now looking a creamy white.
2. For the sauce: melt the butter in a small saucepan, toss in the

herbs and season to taste. Squeeze in the lemon juice and
pour over the hake immediately.
3. Serve garnished with slices of lemon and sprigs of fennel or
   parsley. A good accompaniment would be punchnep (see
   p. 202), a very pretty and tasty dish.

M   Suitable for microwave cookery (do not use foil)

F   Not suitable for freezing

AP Prepare and wrap the hake. Make up the sauce then cover

Skate with sorrel sauce

Cath for gyda saws suran

More skate is brought into Milford Haven on trawlers than any other fish. Sold at the colourful, early-morning fish market, much is cleaned and gutted at the quayside before being transported nationwide.

Skate isn't always easy to find at the fishmonger's, but if you do find some there is no better way to serve it than with this tangy sorrel sauce. It is simplicity itself, and I recommend that you make up as much sauce as you can so that any left over can be used with a variety of pork, chicken or fish dishes.

800 g (1 lb 12 oz) skate wing –
    ask your fishmonger to
    chop it into 4 portions
1 tbsp wine vinegar

For the sauce
2 handfuls freshly picked
    sorrel

1 tsp fresh lovage or sage,
    chopped
125 g (5 oz) unsalted butter
150 ml (5 fl oz) double cream
lemon juice to taste
salt and freshly ground black
    pepper

1. Rinse the skate portions well and place in a shallow pan with water to cover and the vinegar. Bring to the boil, lower the heat, cover and simmer very gently for 20 minutes.
2. For the sauce: wash and chop the sorrel and cook over a low heat with the lovage in just 12 g (½ oz) of the butter for about one minute until dark green and soft. Dice the remaining butter and in a separate pan heat gently to melt (it must not separate). Add the cream and heat the mixture without letting it boil.
3. Take the sauce off the heat and beat in a good squeeze of lemon juice to thicken it, then add the sorrel and lovage. Season to taste.

4. Remove the black skin from the skate and serve on the bone with the sauce passed separately.

M   Not suitable for microwave cookery

F   Not suitable for freezing

AP Prepare the ingredients so that the entire dish can be cooked in just 20 minutes by poaching the skate and cooking the sauce at the same time

Sewin with Pembroke sauce
Sewin gyda saws Penfro

Sewin, or sea trout, is a great favourite with the Welsh and is in season from March until the end of August. The pretty pink flesh and delicate flavour should not be drowned by too strong a sauce, therefore this mild green mayonnaise is the perfect accompaniment. This dish of a whole cold sewin would be ideal for a picnic or a summer party. For a family meal why not use salmon or sewin steaks instead?

900 g (2 lb) sewin (sea trout), complete with head, cleaned
50 g (2 oz) butter
1 tsp parsley, chopped
1 tsp dill, chopped
juice of 1 lemon

For the sauce
1½ handfuls fresh spinach leaves
1 bunch fresh watercress
1 handful parsley
2 tbsp chervil, chopped

1 tsp dill, chopped
150 ml (5 fl oz) homemade (see p. 20) or good-quality bought mayonnaise
salt and freshly ground black pepper
2 tsp fresh lemon juice
150 ml (5 fl oz) double cream, whipped

To garnish
slices of cucumber
sprigs of watercress

1. Wrap the sewin in a large piece of well-buttered foil with the fresh herbs, lemon juice and remaining butter cut into slivers. Seal the foil tightly and bake in a moderate oven (gas 4, 350°F, 180°C) for 25–30 minutes (allow approximately 20 minutes for steaks). Test by piercing the flesh at the thickest part – if it has set into flakes then it is cooked. (Another

simple test is to check that the eye of the fish has turned white.)

2. Allow the fish to cool in the foil before carefully peeling off the skin. Remove the fin and trim the tail into a fork shape, then place the sewin on an oval serving dish.

3. For the sauce: place the spinach, watercress and herbs in a very little boiling water and simmer gently till tender – about 2 minutes. Strain and squeeze out the water. Put the herbs in a liquidizer and blend till smooth.

4. Fold the herbs into the mayonnaise, add seasoning and lemon juice to taste, and finally fold in the whipped cream.

5. Serve the sewin with a garnish of cucumber and watercress, and pass the sauce separately.

M A whole fish will not cook evenly in a microwave, but sewin steaks can be adjusted to microwave cookery

F Not suitable for freezing

AP Prepare the fish completely, arrange on a plate, cover with damp greaseproof paper and keep in the fridge until required. Prepare the sauce and cover with clingfilm, pressing it right down on to the surface of the sauce to stop any skin or blemishes forming

Bard's fish dish
Pysgodyn y bardd

This is one of several versions of a recipe known to the Romans as *Egardoucye*, and popular throughout the Middle Ages when it was a favourite way of making fairly tough fish deliciously palatable on fish days. It is particularly suitable for freshwater fish, when a little added flavour can be a good thing, but the recipe adapts well to sea fish too. The combination of honey, spices and vinegar is fairly pungent but doesn't detract from the delicate flavour of the fish, in fact rather the opposite, it enhances it. Roger Worsley, who gave me this recipe, delights in dishes with a history as he demonstrates in his enchanting series 'Tastes of the Times' which appears in the *Pembrokeshire Magazine*.

900 g–1.15 k (2–2½ lb) perch, pike, freshwater bream, or any fish of your choice, gutted, boned and skinned (see p. 18) – or buy 675 g (1½ lb) fillets
seasoned flour
3 tbsp olive oil
3 tbsp honey

175 ml (6 fl oz) wine vinegar
1 medium onion, minced
2–4 cloves
pinch of mace
salt and freshly ground black pepper

To garnish
2 tbsp fresh chervil, chopped

1. Cut the fish into 5 cm (2 in) cubes and roll them in the seasoned flour.
2. Heat the oil in a frying pan and fry the fish briskly until crisp and golden brown.
3. Place the fish in a deep ovenproof dish and add the honey, vinegar, onion, cloves, mace and seasoning. Cover and cook gently in a warm oven (gas 3, 325°F, 170°C) for 30–45

minutes depending on what type of fish you are using. Serve straight from the dish garnished with the fresh chervil, and with lots of fresh bread to soak up the juices.

M   Microwave at stage 3

F   Not recommended – flavour of sauce will deteriorate

AP Prepare in advance. Cook later

Devilled crab

Crancod y diafol

Crabs are plentiful around the south-west coast of Wales. As a camper in the small seaside village of Newport, Pembrokeshire, I recall that one of the greatest pleasures was to buy freshly boiled crabs from the little fish stall on the harbour front. This small fishing community brought in a daily catch of lobster, skate, rock salmon, pollock and mackerel, and for the keen holidaymaker trips out with the fishermen were pure heaven.

The richness of crabmeat, both white and brown, adds a touch of luxury to any seafood dish. Preparing a crab is not a difficult job and it takes no more than 20 minutes for a complete novice to extract the flesh from a freshly cooked crab. But if you don't have the time or patience to prepare a whole crab in its shell, then buy some crabmeat from the fishmonger.

1 tbsp anchovy essence
2 tsp soy sauce
1 tsp Worcestershire sauce
¼ tsp Tabasco
juice of ½ lemon
salt and freshly ground black
   pepper
450 g (1 lb) crabmeat (both
   white and brown mixed)

225 ml (8 fl oz) double cream
50 g (2 oz) fresh breadcrumbs
50 g (2 oz) Cheddar cheese,
   grated

To garnish
lemon wedges

1. In a medium-sized saucepan, mix the anchovy essence, soy sauce, Worcestershire sauce, Tabasco, lemon juice and seasoning. Add the crabmeat and heat to boiling. Remove from heat and add enough cream to produce a thick sauce consistency.
2. Transfer the mixture to a shallow ovenproof dish, or back to

the original crab shell, and top with the breadcrumbs and cheese.
3. Place under a moderately hot grill until golden brown. Garnish with lemon wedges.
- This is a very rich dish and should be served with a bowl of buttered fresh pasta or a simple purée of potatoes, piped in a border round the dish, and a crisp green salad.

M Prepare the recipe up to stage 2 in a microwave

F Not suitable for freezing

AP Luckily this is a very quick dish to prepare, but if desperate to get ahead then work up to the end of stage 2 in advance

Cockles and pasta
Cocos gyda phasta

Today pasta is available throughout Britain. Filling, cheap and quick to prepare, it is a favourite meal with almost everyone. But pasta came to Wales some time ago with the large immigrant Italian population who arrived to open cafés in the valleys during the boom years of coal mining. If there is an argument against pasta meals, it is that they lack texture and flavour, but this recipe has both with a touch of luxury too.

350 g (12 oz) tagliatelle
6 rashers streaky bacon, cut into strips
1 medium onion, finely chopped
1 clove garlic, crushed with salt
225 g (8 oz) cooked fresh cockles
2 tbsp parsley, chopped

150 ml (5 fl oz) dry white wine
salt and lots of freshly ground black pepper
300 ml (10 fl oz) cream, single or double

To serve
freshly grated Parmesan cheese

1. Cook the tagliatelle in a large pan of boiling salted water with 1 tbsp cooking oil.
2. Meanwhile, make the sauce: in a medium-sized saucepan or heavy-based casserole dish gently fry the bacon strips without any added fat. Once the bacon fat begins to run add the onion and garlic and cook briskly until the onion is almost soft but not brown.
3. Stir in the cockles, parsley, white wine and seasoning, bring to the boil and stir in the cream. Heat through.
4. Drain the cooked tagliatelle through a colander, rinse with hot water to prevent it sticking together and arrange in a

large serving bowl. Pour over the cockle sauce, mix well, and hand the Parmesan cheese separately.

M   Ideal for the microwave

F   This is one of those dishes that is quicker to cook from raw than cook from the freezer

AP This meal takes only 15 minutes to prepare from start to finish and tastes wonderful served fresh from the stove

Aberaeron mackerel

Macrell aberaeron

No visitor to the west coast of Wales should miss the chance to taste the fare at the Hive on the Quay at Aberaeron. This pretty fishing port boasts two specialities, mackerel and bees, and you can eat one and see the other at the Hive on the Quay. The bees are displayed in observation hives and after a tour of the small Bee Museum you can eat superb food in the restaurant. This simple dish of soused mackerel gives the fish a spicy tang and enhances their flavour.

4 good-sized fresh mackerel, cleaned and gutted
1 large onion, cut into rings

For the marinade
6 bay leaves
3 dried chillies
1 tsp black peppercorns

6 cloves
1 tsp salt
400 ml (13 fl oz) wine vinegar
200 ml (7 fl oz) water

To garnish
chopped chives or parsley

1. Lay the fish head to tail in an ovenproof dish.
2. Mix together the marinade ingredients and pour over the fish, adding more water if necessary to cover. Sprinkle over the onion rings, cover with foil and bake in a moderate oven (gas 4, 350°F, 180°C) for 20–25 minutes, or until the eyes of the fish go white.
3. Leave the mackerel to cool in the dish, then remove the foil and scatter fresh parsley or chopped chives over the top to serve.
• A salad made from freshly boiled potatoes dressed whilst still hot with a sharp vinaigrette goes well with the mackerel.

M   Suitable for microwave cookery (do not use foil)

F   Not suitable for freezing

AP Cook a day in advance and leave to cool overnight in the fridge

Trout cooked in leeks

Brithyll mewn cennin

'And there is good fresh trout for supper. My mother used to put them on a hot stone over the fire, wrapped in breadcrumbs, butter, parsley and lemon rind, all bound about with the fresh leaves of leeks. If there is better food in heaven, I am in a hurry to be there.' A magical quote from *How Green Was My Valley*, Richard Llewellyn.

4 good-sized fresh trout, gutted and cleaned – if you prefer you may remove the backbone (see p. 18)
2 tsp fresh parsley, chopped
salt and freshly ground black pepper

8 large leek leaves, but not tough ones
8 rashers of streaky bacon, derinded

To garnish
lemon wedges
sprigs of parsley

1. Sprinkle some parsley, salt and pepper into the cavity of each fish.
2. Wash the leek leaves and wrap two round each trout. Surround the leeks with the bacon and secure with a cocktail stick if necessary. Place the fish close together on a baking tray.
3. Bake in a moderate oven (gas 4, 350°F, 180°C) for 20 minutes, or until the bacon is crisp and the trout cooked inside (check to see if the flesh flakes apart when prodded gently with the tip of a knife).
4. Garnish each trout with a sprig of parsley and a wedge of lemon and serve immediately.

M   Cook in the microwave but transfer to a preheated grill to brown the bacon at the last minute

F   Not suitable for freezing

AP Prepare up to the end of stage 2

Mackerel with oranges
Macrell gydag oren

If you should ever go to Anglesey do make sure to visit the Sea Zoo at Brynsiencyn, where not only can you see fish from local waters – from conger eels six feet long, live lobsters, hermit crabs, sea bass and, of course, sea-green mackerel – but you also have the chance to touch the fish too!

Fresh mackerel straight from the sea have a unique taste for, alas, within an hour or so the sweetness and delicate texture will deteriorate. Always choose firm-to-touch fish with brilliant sea-green colours, at their best from late June to early September.

To counterbalance the oiliness of the flesh I suggest you serve an acid fruit marinade, such as the one below, with your mackerel.

4 medium-sized mackerel, cleaned and gutted

For the marinade
2 tbsp sunflower or vegetable oil
grated rind and juice of 2 oranges
few drops Tabasco

salt and freshly ground black pepper
1 tbsp fresh dill, finely chopped

To garnish
orange slices, cut in half and twisted over the mackerel

1. Make slanting incisions with a sharp knife across both sides of each fish. Place in an ovenproof dish.
2. Mix together the ingredients for the marinade and pour over the fish. Leave for two hours, turning occasionally.
3. Place the fish on a grill pan. Grill for 5–8 minutes on each

side, brushing with marinade. When cooked place on a
serving dish and pour over the juices from the grill pan.
4. Garnish the mackerel with the fresh orange, and serve with
chunks of fresh granary bread and a glass of cider.

M   Not suitable for microwave cookery

F   Not suitable for freezing

AP Prepare up to the end of stage 2, marinate overnight if you
prefer and then grill just before serving

Roulade of fresh salmon, with an avocado and smoked salmon filling

Rholyn eog

This is just the type of delicious dish that Michael Lewis will prepare for you when you visit Wolfscastle Country Hotel. Michael's fame is spreading through Dyfed and the hotel now arranges gourmet evenings at least once a month for Michael to exhibit his prowess.

Both the fresh and smoked salmon served at the Wolfscastle Country Hotel come from Cenarth, where salmon leap in the river and the unlucky ones end up hanging in the chimney of the nearby smokery.

For the roulade
225 g (8 oz) fresh salmon, weighed when cooked and flaked
4 eggs, separated
75 ml (3 fl oz) double cream, whipped
salt and freshly ground black pepper
1–2 tsp Parmesan cheese, freshly grated

For the filling
2 avocado pears
100 g (4 oz) smoked salmon, diced
100 g (4 oz) ricotta or curd cheese
1 tsp fresh dill, chopped

1. First prepare a 25 cm × 20 cm (10 in × 8 in) Swiss roll tin by lining it with Bakewell or parchment paper. Take care over the corners and make sure that the paper comes up at least 2.5 cm (1 in) above the rim.
2. For the roulade, mash the cooked salmon with a fork, fold in the egg yolks and whipped cream and season to taste.
3. Whisk the egg whites till stiff and fold into the salmon with half the Parmesan.

4. Spread the roulade mixture evenly over the Swiss roll tin and dust with the remaining Parmesan cheese. Bake in a hot oven (gas 7, 425°F, 220°C) for 10–15 minutes until firm to the touch.

5. Meanwhile, for the filling, mash the avocado flesh, mix with the smoked salmon, ricotta and fresh dill.

6. Once the roulade is out of the oven, leave to cool for 5 minutes then turn on to a sheet of Bakewell paper. Carefully peel off the old paper, quickly spread the filling over the roulade and roll up. If this sounds too daunting, simply spread the filling down one of the long sides of the roulade and fold the other side on top. Slide the roulade on to a serving dish and serve at once.

● This is a very rich dish and needs nothing more than a simple salad and some fresh bread with it.

M   Not suitable for microwave cookery

F   Not suitable for freezing

AP Make up the filling and cover with clingfilm, pressing right down on to the surface of the mixture. Prepare the roulade up to the end of stage 2. Finish at time of serving

Sea bass with garlic sauce
Draenogiaid y mor mewn saws garlleg

Sea bass are found in great numbers off the Llyn Peninsula, around Anglesey and in the Menai Straights, and should you visit North Wales it is more than likely that you will be offered fresh sea bass at any good restaurant. The idea for this recipe came from Nerys Roberts, who takes enormous care to present local foods, beautifully cooked, to her customers at Y Bistro in Llanberis.

Sea bass is a superb fish to cook, with good firm flesh that holds together well, and a pleasure to eat for its fine flavour and lack of bones.

1 large sea bass weighing 1.15 kg (2½ lb), scaled and gutted (or use 4 small sea bass weighing 225–350 g (½–¾ lb)	large bunch of parsley 6 cloves garlic 100 g (4 oz) butter salt and freshly ground black pepper

1. Wash the sea bass well under the cold tap, cut three slits in each side of the fish and slip a sliver of garlic into each. Place half the parsley and another clove of garlic inside the fish and brush the skin with butter.
2. Wrap the sea bass in buttered foil, place on a baking tray and bake in a moderate oven (gas 4, 350°F, 180°C) for 15–20 minutes depending on size. The fish is cooked if the flesh breaks into flakes when pierced with a knife.
3. To make the sauce, melt the butter in a small pan, chop the two remaining garlic cloves finely and cook them in the butter until they are just beginning to colour and the butter has turned a healthy brown. (Take care it doesn't burn, though.)

4. Serve the bass straight from the oven. Lift it carefully off the foil and on to a large serving dish, pour the sauce over and garnish with the remaining parsley, finely chopped.

● This is a powerful dish and needs lots and lots of deliciously crisp French bread to soak up the garlic juices.

M   Suitable for microwave cookery

F   Not suitable for freezing

AP Have all the ingredients prepared, but cook at the last minute

Scallops in gin
Cregyn cylchog meddw

Lucky scallops, soaked in gin! In fact the alcohol will be burnt away when it is flamed and just the aromatic flavour of the juniper berries in the gin is left. This dish is a pretty pink and I suggest that you serve it surrounded by saffron rice – a tempting colour combination even for those with the most jaded of palates. Very rich in flavour, this recipe adapts well to being served in smaller portions as a starter.

50 g (2 oz) butter
8–12 fresh scallops (depending on size), shelled and cleaned
1 small onion, finely chopped
4 juniper berries, crushed with a rolling pin or in a mortar
4 tbsp gin
2 tsp tomato purée
juice of ½ a lemon
300 ml (10 fl oz) single cream (use *crème fraîche* if you prefer, but adjust the lemon juice so that the sauce isn't too sharp)

salt and freshly ground black pepper

To garnish
lemon wedges
sprigs of watercress
a few juniper berries which have been soaked in boiling water for 5 minutes to soften

To serve
saffron rice (see below)

1. In a large frying pan melt the butter and fry the scallops for one minute on either side. Remove from the pan and keep warm. Add the onion to the same pan and cook gently until transparent.
2. Add the crushed juniper berries and the gin and flame by

igniting the warm gin in the pan and allowing the alcohol to burn off. Once the flame has gone out continue to cook until almost all the gin has evaporated.

3. Return the scallops to the pan, add the tomato purée, lemon juice, cream and seasoning and simmer gently until it has thickened slightly, but not too long or the scallops will toughen.

4. Serve the scallops on a bed of saffron rice garnished with the soaked juniper berries, sprigs of watercress and lemon wedges.

• Saffron rice: Soak 1 pkt saffron strands or ¼ tsp saffron powder in 3 tbsp hot water for 10 minutes. In a heavy-based casserole melt 25 g (1 oz) butter. Cook 1 small, finely chopped onion gently for 5 minutes then toss in 225 g (8 oz) long grain patna rice. Stir, and fry for 3 minutes until the rice changes from transparent to a whitish colour. Pour in 450 ml (¾ pint) hot chicken stock. Season and add the saffron water. Cover the casserole and bake in a moderate oven (gas 4, 350°F, 180°C) for 15–18 minutes, until the rice is cooked and all the stock is absorbed. (Add a little boiling water if the rice gets too dry.)

M   Don't flame the scallops in the microwave! But do prepare the rice in it

F   The sauce may separate in the freezer, but the rice will freeze well for a limited period, say a month

AP   Prepare the rice in advance, reheat, covered, in a moderate oven (gas 4, 350°F, 180°C) for 20 minutes or in the microwave

Fisherman's pie
Pastai'r pysgotwr

Haven't we all got a recipe for fish pie? Well, if not then try this one because it is different and rather special, spiced with Worcestershire sauce and cayenne pepper with just a hint of Caerphilly cheese. For my fish I visit Ashton's in Cardiff's Central Market. This fishmonger has a regular clientele which demands everything from fresh tuna, squid, swordfish, live eels, bogue, jack fish and live clams to fresh sardines and salmon heads. With more than sixty varieties of fresh fish on sale at any one time it is not surprising that Ashton's is an award-winning fishmonger.

450 g (1 lb) white fish fillets
300 ml (½ pint) milk
salt and freshly ground black
   pepper
1 bay leaf
25 g (1 oz) butter
1 small onion, chopped
25 g (1 oz) flour
½ tsp dry mustard
1 dsp Worcestershire sauce

½ tsp cayenne pepper
50 g (2 oz) Caerphilly cheese,
   grated
450 g (1 lb) creamed potato
   (boiled potatoes mashed
   with butter, milk and
   seasoning)

To garnish
chopped parsley

1. Put the fish in an ovenproof dish with the milk, salt, pepper and bay leaf. Cover and bake for 20 minutes in a moderate oven (gas 4, 350°F, 180°C) until fish is tender. Cool in the liquid then lift out (retaining the liquid), remove skin and bones and flake the fish. (This is a much more gentle way to cook fish than boiling it on top of the stove.)
2. Melt the butter in a pan, fry the onion gently until transparent, then stir in the flour and dry mustard and cook for 2

minutes over low heat. Add the milk in which the fish was cooked made up to 300 ml (½ pint) if necessary with more milk. Bring to the boil, stirring constantly until sauce thickens.

3. Season, add the Worcestershire sauce and cayenne pepper, then stir in the grated cheese until it melts. Mix in the flaked fish and transfer to a buttered ovenproof dish.

4. Cover with the creamed potatoes, level off and mark with the back of a fork. Bake on the top shelf of a fairly hot oven (gas 6, 400°F, 200°C) for about 15 minutes.

5. Garnish the pie with chopped parsley and serve with fresh vegetables or a crisp salad.

M   All parts of this dish may be cooked in the microwave. Combine and bake or grill to finish

F   Freezes well

AP Prepare the whole dish, chill until required then bake for 30 minutes until hot through and crisp on top

Laverbread, mussel and tomato tart
Tarten bara lawr, cregyn gleision a thomato

This is a dish that I first ate at Bodysgallen Hall just outside Llandudno in the extreme north of Wales. All vegetables and herbs served in the dining room are grown in their own walled vegetable garden but alas they can't supply their own seaweed and shellfish. Local fishermen are reliable, though, and can guarantee deliveries of the local sea specialities. If you can't buy laverbread then use cooked spinach in the same quantities.

For the rich shortcrust pastry
175 g (6 oz) flour
75 g (3 oz) butter or firm
  margarine
1 egg yolk
1 tbsp water

For the filling
1 medium onion, chopped
25 g (1 oz) butter

100 g (4 oz) laverbread,
  prepared and cooked
100 g (4 oz) cooked mussels
175 ml (6 fl oz) creamy milk,
  or half milk and half cream
1 egg and 1 yolk, beaten
salt and freshly ground black
  pepper
1 tbsp fresh parsley, chopped
2 tomatoes, sliced

1. Make the pastry, chill for 30 minutes, then roll out and use to line a 20 cm (8 in) flan case.
2. Fry the onion gently in the butter for 5 minutes until soft. Combine it with the laverbread, mussels, milk, beaten eggs and seasoning.
3. Pour the filling into the flan case, sprinkle the parsley over the surface and arrange the tomatoes on top.
4. Bake in a hot oven (gas 7–8, 425–450°F, 220–230°C) for the first 10 minutes to set the pastry then turn the heat down and cook in a moderate oven (gas 4, 350°F, 180°C) for another 20 minutes. Serve warm for maximum flavour.

M   Not suitable for microwave cookery

F   The tart is best frozen filled but uncooked. Cook from frozen

AP Make and cook in advance. Reheat in a very low oven to serve

POULTRY AND GAME

Pigeon pie
Pheasant with apples
Stuffed guinea fowl
Roast Pembrokeshire duck with whinberry
    sauce
Chicken with plums
Chicken breasts with Welsh farmhouse
    Cheddar
Abergavenny chicken
Chicken kebabs with blackberry sauce
Hare in red wine
Roast duck with honey, lemon and mint
    sauce
Dark Age chicken
Venison pie
Goose with apple stuffing
Salt duck
Rabbit with damsons
Welsh chicken pie

Poultry is in fashion now as never before. Easily digestible white meat with a low fat content, it's just what the doctor ordered. But has our desire for cheap chicken overshadowed the basic quality of what we eat? The flavour has gone out of poultry, and many of us accept flavourless frozen chicken into our diets without a murmur. Fresh, free-range birds are now available from various outlets and the firmness of the flesh combined with the flavour are a great improvement. You must expect to pay for this privilege though.

It wasn't so long ago that chickens scratched about in most farmyards and rural smallholdings throughout Britain, enjoying freedom and a varied diet that only added to the flavour of their flesh. If today we have little choice but to eat modern poultry products then more thought and care must go into their cooking. Chicken is now common to almost all our diets since it is inexpensive and one of the easiest meals to prepare. Gone are the days where a roast chicken on Sunday was a rare delicacy, something to really look forward to.

So think carefully when buying chicken. No doubt the texture will be soft and acceptable to your palate, but will there be enough flavour? If not, add some. It needn't be anything too extravagant; chicken with plums, apples, honey or wine – all these combinations taste delicious and are straightforward to prepare.

Fresh, farm-reared geese are relatively easy to come by and are still eaten a great deal in Wales. They have always played an important part in Welsh rural life. An aggressive, territorial creature, the goose rules the farmyard and has often been used in place of a guard dog. Not only are they a favourite bird for Christmas dinner but the feathers are used to make down pillows and quilts and the wing pinion was at one time used as a hearth brush. Goose flesh tends to be rather fatty, so choose a recipe with a tang to it, such as goose with apples, which will set off its flavour.

Game suffers from not being fatty enough and care must be taken not to let rabbit, hare, venison or any of the game birds dry out during cooking. The Celtic method of cooking meat in a stew is ideal for game, ensuring that the flesh stays moist and its flavour blends with the liquid to make a superb sauce. Wine makes perhaps the best sauce for dark-fleshed game, so next time you have hare or some venison destined for the pot, do add a bottle of red wine.

Lastly, if you are feeling adventurous, try Lady Llanover's recipe for salt duck (p. 145). Preparations must start two days in advance, but the end result is really worth tasting, so why not savour a flavour from the past?

Pigeon pie
Pastai 'sguthan

Not for high days and holidays this meal of pigeon pie, more a case of catch as catch can. Game such as hare, pigeon and pheasant added variety to the limited diet of rural Welsh people, as did trout pulled from the rivers or cockles gathered on the shore.

I love the richness of pigeon, especially when it is cooked slowly to add flavour to the sauce. Make your own rough puff pastry; it's dead easy and much much more delicious than any packet you can buy.

2 plump pigeons, plucked and drawn
1 bay leaf
sprig of wild thyme or 1 tsp dried thyme
25 g (1 oz) butter
1 medium onion, sliced
100 g (4 oz) mushrooms, chopped (large field ones if possible)
1 tbsp flour
100 ml (4 fl oz) red wine

salt and freshly ground black pepper
100 g (4 oz) dried prunes, soaked overnight in cold tea

For the rough puff pastry
225 g (8 oz) plain flour
pinch of salt
175 g (6 oz) butter or firm margarine
150 ml (¾ pint) iced water

1. First prepare the pastry: sift the flour and salt into a large bowl, then add the butter, cut into cherry-sized lumps. Using a palette knife cut the butter into the flour until all the lumps are well covered. Pour in all the water and stir briskly with the knife to combine the ingredients. Tip the lumpy-looking dough on to a floured table and roll it out to an oblong 25 cm × 13 cm (10 in × 5 in). Fold the top third of

pastry down and the bottom third up. Give the dough a half turn through 45 degrees and roll out again to a large rectangle. Fold and roll again so that, in all, the pastry will have been turned 3 times. Now chill for an hour.

2. Wash the pigeons inside and out then put them side by side in a large saucepan and cover with water. Add the bay leaf and thyme and bring to the boil. Simmer for about 45 minutes, maybe twice as long, depending on the age and toughness of the pigeons. Test by gently pulling at a leg to see if it is ready to come away from the carcass. Once cooked, leave the pigeons to cool in the liquid.

3. Melt the butter in a saucepan, fry the onion gently for 3 minutes before adding the chopped mushrooms, cook for 1 minute then stir in the flour. Cook again for 1 minute then gradually add the wine and approximately 300 ml (½ pint) cooking stock from the pigeons. Season and boil up well for 3 minutes.

4. Cut the pigeon flesh from the carcasses and add it to the sauce together with the soaked and stoned prunes. Pour into a 1.2 l (2 pint) pie dish.

5. Roll out the pastry to cover the top of the pie, damp the edges to help them stick to the dish and make a steam vent in the middle. Brush with a little beaten egg and bake for 30–40 minutes in a moderately hot oven (gas 6, 400°F, 200°C) until crisp and golden.

M   Cook the pigeons in the microwave, but not the pie

F   Freeze the cooked pigeon in the sauce and the prepared pastry raw

AP Prepare up to the end of stage 4

Pheasant with apples

Ffesant gydag afalau

Earlier this century, farming communities in rural Wales much appreciated the occasional addition of a pheasant to their basic diet. In times of hardship any produce from the farm or smallholding was sold off to provide a little extra income. Eggs, cream and chickens would be sold or exchanged within the local community and often there wasn't much left for the family. Not that all lucky catches of game brought tender juicy meals; old birds do get tough, and if you are in doubt about the age of your pheasant, this is an ideal way to soften up an old bird.

1 plump pheasant, jointed (see instructions for chicken on p. 17)	35 g (1½ oz) butter
	1 medium onion, sliced
	2 sticks celery, chopped
1 bay leaf	2 medium cooking apples,
sprig of parsley or any fresh herbs to hand	peeled, cored and chopped
	150 ml (5 fl oz) cider
salt and freshly ground black pepper	2 tbsp Calvados (optional)
	75 ml (3 fl oz) double cream
2–3 tbsp flour	

1. Put the pheasant carcass, the neck and cleaned giblets into a large pan, together with the bay leaf, fresh herbs and seasoning. Cover with cold water, bring to the boil and simmer gently for about 30 minutes.
2. Coat the pheasant joints lightly with flour and fry them briskly in the butter in a heavy-based casserole until brown on all sides.
3. Remove the pheasant joints and lower the heat under the casserole. Fry the onion and celery for 5 minutes then add the chopped apple and fry for another 5 minutes.

4. Stir in enough of the remaining flour to absorb the butter in the pan (about 1 tbsp) then blend in the cider, Calvados and 300 ml (½ pint) of the pheasant stock. Bring to the boil.
5. Replace the pheasant joints and add more stock if necessary so that the joints are almost covered. Season to taste and cover the casserole. Cook in a warm oven (gas 3, 325°F, 170°C) for 45 minutes or until the pheasant is tender.
6. Stir in the cream, and serve the pheasant from the casserole. If the sauce needs thickening, remove the joints from the casserole, boil up the liquid to reduce and thicken it, then add the cream.

M   Cook to end of stage 5 in the microwave

F   Freeze in a deep container so that the sauce covers all the pheasant joints to prevent them drying out. Thaw completely before reheating

AP Make in advance. Reheat gently when required

Stuffed guinea fowl

Ceiliog brith wedi'i stwffio

This is a dream of a dish for a dinner party. Guinea fowl has rather a special flavour but not enough flesh to make it an 'easy' eat. By taking the bones out and rolling the bird around the stuffing you are left with a manageable and delicious meal. Two guinea fowl may be too much for four people but one will probably be too little, and anyway it will taste delicious cold the next day.

2 guinea fowl, boned (ask your butcher to do it and give you the bones)
sprig of any fresh herb
100 g (4 oz) dried apricots
50 g (2 oz) walnuts, halved
1 tbsp fresh chervil or thyme, chopped
2 tbsp pine kernels

For the sauce
juice of 2 oranges
2 tbsp redcurrant jelly
100 ml (4 fl oz) port or Madeira
a good pinch of nutmeg
salt and freshly ground black pepper

To garnish
orange slices

1. Put the bones in a large pan, cover with water and simmer for 2 hours with a sprig of herbs. Strain off the liquid and boil it hard to reduce the stock to 300 ml (½ pint).
2. Place a row of dried apricots and walnuts down the centre of the boned birds, sprinkle over the chervil or thyme and pine kernels then fold both sides over and tie the birds in 5 places – 4 across and 1 lengthways.
3. Bake the guinea fowl side by side, covered with buttered foil, in a hot oven (gas 7, 425°F, 220°C) for 45 minutes.
4. For the sauce: in a small sauce pan combine the orange juice,

redcurrant jelly, port and nutmeg with the stock made from the guinea fowl carcasses and simmer for 10 minutes. Season to taste.

5. Serve the guinea fowl sliced and garnished with the orange. Hand the sauce separately.

M   Suitable for microwave cookery (don't use foil)

F   Freeze the birds whole, well covered. Don't freeze the sauce

AP   Prepare the recipe up to the end of stage 2. Make up the sauce in advance

Roast Pembrokeshire duck with whinberry sauce

Hwyaden sir benfro mewn saws llus

Whinberries, as the Welsh call them, are variously known throughout the British Isles as wortleberries, blaeberries or bilberries. In season in late August and throughout September, these berries colour the open countryside and your search will be best rewarded in the north-east corner of Wales on the lower slopes of Snowdonia, or else search the Presilli mountains in Dyfed. For those walking the Pembrokeshire coastal route, there will no doubt be sustenance in the form of juicy berries *en route*.

1 large domestic duck
  1.8–2.25 k (4–5 lb) or 2 wild
  ducks
salt and freshly ground black
  pepper
25–50 g (1–2 oz) butter

For the whinberry sauce
225 g (8 oz) whinberries
2 tbsp redcurrant jelly
juice of 1 orange
100 ml (4 fl oz) red wine
3 cardamom pods

1. Sprinkle the duck with pepper and salt then spread a little butter over the breast. Roast in a hot oven (gas 7, 425°F, 220°C) allowing 15 minutes per pound of the trussed bird's weight. Baste frequently to obtain a good crisp skin.
2. To make up the sauce, pick over the whinberries then cover them with cold water in a small saucepan and simmer until soft, about 5 minutes. Add the redcurrant jelly, orange juice, red wine and ground seeds from the cardamom pods and simmer for another 5 minutes.
3. Sieve the sauce, pressing the berries with the back of a wooden spoon to extract all the flavour.
4. To carve the duck cut the crackling skin with the point of a sharp knife and cut the meat from the breast in thin, long slivers along the bone. To find the wing joints is no easy

task; use carving secateurs or scissors to save time and
temper. Serve the duck with the sauce handed separately.

M   Suitable for microwave cookery, but crisp the duck skin in
a conventional oven or under the grill after cooking

F   Freeze the duck either whole or cut into slices. Freeze the
sauce separately

AP Roast the duck a little ahead of time, it won't hurt to sit in a
warm oven for 15 minutes before carving. Prepare the sauce
in advance

Chicken with plums
Cyw iar efo eirin

Plums, garlic and parsley – an unusual combination, you may think, but if you have ever been overwhelmed by a glut of plums in August, this is the ideal way to deal with them. A health-giving dish, no less, for as well as the fine qualities of garlic let me quote a little herbal lore on parsley from *Welsh Herbal Medicine* by David Hoffman : 'It will stimulate the spirits greatly, and strengthen the stomach.'

450 g (1 lb) fresh red plums
   (substitute tinned red
   plums if necessary)
150 ml (¼ pint) water
4 chicken breasts, skinned
seasoned flour
2 tbsp olive oil
50 g (2 oz) butter

2 cloves garlic
handful of parsley, chopped
salt and freshly ground black
   pepper

To garnish
sprigs of parsley

1. Stew the plums in the water until soft.
2. Toss the chicken breasts in the seasoned flour and fry gently in the oil and butter for 15 minutes, turning after 7 minutes so that both sides are golden brown.
3. Stone the plums and in a liquidizer or food processor blend them with the garlic, parsley and seasoning.
4. Put the cooked chicken in a shallow ovenproof dish, pour over the plum sauce, cover with a lid or foil and cook in a moderate oven (gas 4, 350°F, 180°C) for 30 minutes. Garnish with the parsley.
- The sauce is such a stunning colour that this dish is best served plainly, with just new potatoes and a salad.

M   Ideal for everything except frying the chicken

F   Freezes well, but remember that the garlic will lose some of
     its pungency if frozen for too long

AP   Prepare the recipe up to the end of stage 3

Chicken breasts with Welsh farmhouse Cheddar

Darnau cyw iar gyda chaws ffermdy cymreig

Chicken and cheese make a fine combination of tastes and textures. The cheese not only adds a good flavour but also a juiciness to the rather dry flesh of a chicken breast. This dish is simple to prepare but smart in presentation. Welsh Cheddar has a sharp and nutty flavour; if it isn't available I suggest you use a mature farmhouse Cheddar instead.

4 good-sized chicken breasts, skin and bones removed
50 g (2 oz) Welsh farmhouse Cheddar, cut into 4 strips
1 tbsp wholegrain mustard (Welsh, if possible)

1 tbsp parsley, finely chopped
4 rashers streaky bacon, de-rinded
25 g (1 oz) butter
juice of ½ lemon

1. Cut a slit in the side of each chicken breast and stuff with a slice of cheese, some mustard and parsley.
2. Wrap a rasher of bacon around each breast and secure with a cocktail stick to keep the two together.
3. Pack the chicken close together in a baking tin or open casserole and bake in a hot oven (gas 6, 400°F, 200°C) for 20 minutes, or until the bacon is crisp and the chicken cooked right through. Remove the cocktail sticks.
4. Heat the butter in a small saucepan and when it starts to sizzle, add the lemon juice. Pour over the finished chicken.

- Serve with a potato and onion cake (see p. 221) and a fresh green vegetable.
- Instead of chicken breasts, whole legs or large chicken thighs could be used. Bone the joints by scraping the flesh away from the bone with a small sharp knife. Don't worry if it looks untidy; just wrap the flesh neatly around the filling,

cover with the bacon and secure as normal. The cooked joints will look just as good as the breasts, and cost so much less.

M Microwave the chicken covered to retain the moisture. Crisp the bacon under the grill just before serving

F Freeze the chicken well wrapped, but don't freeze the sauce. Thaw completely before reheating

AP Prepare up to the end of stage 2

Abergavenny chicken
Cyw iar y fenni

'No better cider does the world supply/than grows along thy border, gentle Wye', wrote Edward Davies in his poem on Chepstow of 1786. It is true that in 1899, of the 6,515 apple orchards in Wales 4,035 were in Monmouth, an area famed for the excellence of its eating and cider apples.

4 chicken breasts
300 ml (½ pint) dry cider
1 large leek, cut into
  matchstick slivers
50 g (2 oz) butter
1 large cooking apple, peeled,
  cored and chopped

50 ml (2 fl oz) single cream
salt and freshly ground black
  pepper

To serve
fruity rice (see below)

1. If you have time, soak the chicken breasts in the cider for a couple of hours. Drain the chicken, pat dry on kitchen paper and reserve the cider for the sauce.
2. Blanch the strips of leek by covering with cold water in a saucepan, bringing to the boil and simmering for 1 minute. Drain and rinse in a sieve or colander under the cold tap to set their bright green colour.
3. Melt the butter in a heavy-based frying pan and fry the chicken breasts for 5 minutes on each side. Add the chopped apple and cider and cook for another 10 minutes until the apple flesh is pulpy.
4. Pour in the cream, season to taste and add the strips of leek. Serve with fruity rice.
- To make the fruity rice, bring a large pan of salted water to the boil, add a good slice of lemon for flavour, ¼ tsp turmeric for colour and 225 g (8 oz) long grain rice. Boil

vigorously uncovered for 12 minutes, then test for tender-
ness. Drain in a colander and pour some hot water through
the rice to allow the starch water to drain out. Let the cooked
rice sit in the colander for 15 minutes to dry out a little then
arrange in a buttered, heatproof dish. Stir in 1 tbsp raisins or
currants and cover with a lid or some buttered foil. Reheat
in a moderate oven (gas 4, 350°F, 180°C) for 20 minutes.

M   Suitable for microwave cookery

F   Not suitable; the cream sauce may separate on reheating

AP Prepare the chicken up to the end of stage 3. Prepare the
rice ahead of time and reheat as suggested

Chicken kebabs with blackberry sauce
Kebabs cyw iar gyda saws mwyar duon

Can Welsh blackberries be better than any others? If you need convincing then visit the briar-filled valleys of mid Wales around Machynlleth in September, but don't forget to bring a great many baskets. In early summer use strawberries, raspberries or even gooseberries for this sauce, and if none of these are available then fall back on a tin of blackcurrants during non-berry winter months.

4 good-sized chicken breasts, or equivalent chicken meat or turkey meat
grated rind and juice of 1 lemon
1 clove garlic, crushed with salt
100 ml (4 fl oz) medium or dry white wine
2 tbsp olive oil
1 tbsp fresh basil or sage

For the sauce
225 g (8 oz) fresh, ripe blackberries
75 ml (3 fl oz) water
1 tbsp honey
2 tbsp white wine or cider vinegar
salt and freshly ground black pepper
lemon juice to baste

To serve
Nutty rice (see below)

1. Cut the chicken into bite-size pieces.
2. Make a marinade by mixing the lemon rind, juice, garlic, white wine, olive oil and herbs. Soak the chicken in this for at least 4 hours.
3. For the sauce, simmer the blackberries in the water until soft. Sieve, then add the honey and vinegar, season to taste with salt, pepper and lemon juice. (Gooseberries should be prepared in this way too, but for strawberries and raspberries,

simply sieve the raw fruit and add the honey and vinegar to taste to the pulp. For tinned blackcurrants, strain off the juice, sieve the berries and add honey, vinegar and enough of the juice to make a tangy sauce.)

4. Thread the marinated chicken chunks on to skewers and barbecue over a not-too-fierce heat. Alternatively, cook under a medium grill, but take care; if the grill is too hot the chicken will char but not cook through.

• Serve the kebabs on a bed of nutty rice: boil 225 g (8 fl oz) patna or brown rice and toss in 50 g (2 oz) cashew nuts and 1 tbsp freshly chopped parsley.

M   Use the microwave to prepare the sauce

F   The sauce will freeze well

AP Marinade the chicken, already threaded on to wooden skewers, in a large polythene container overnight. Make up the sauce in advance

Hare in red wine

Ysgyfarnog mewn gwin coch

Ann Fitzgerald's Farmhouse Kitchen may be off the beaten track but it's well worth searching out. It is situated down a dusty track a mile out of the village of Mathry in Dyfed, and you may call at any time of day to choose from a wide range of fresh-baked foods including bread, pies, cakes, pasties and pizzas. Local delicacies such as fresh crab, lobster, sea trout from the River Teifi, game and local cheeses are served in the small dining room and menus offer a wide choice from vegetarian dishes to Far Eastern cookery. Ann cooks from early till late each day, providing visitors with an enormous range of unusual dishes such as this hare in red wine.

1 hare, jointed
2 tbsp olive oil
1 tbsp flour
salt and freshly ground black
   pepper

For the marinade
1 tbsp olive oil
2 cloves garlic, crushed with
   salt
1 bottle red wine, dry and full
   bodied

1 medium onion, finely
   chopped
1 bay leaf
4 juniper berries
sprig of parsley
sprig of thyme
salt and freshly ground black
   pepper

To garnish
chopped parsley

1. Mix together all the ingredients for the marinade, immerse the hare in it and leave in a covered container in the fridge for 2 days.
2. Lift the hare out of the marinade and dry on kitchen paper.

In a deep, heavy-based casserole sauté the joints in the olive oil until lightly browned; lift out and keep warm.

3. Stir the flour into the oil and cook for 2 minutes, stirring all the time. Pour in the marinade and bring to the boil. Return the hare joints to the pot and add enough water to cover the meat completely. Cover and cook in a slow oven (gas 2, 300°F, 150°C) for approximately 3 hours, or until the hare flesh is so tender that it almost falls off the bone.

4. Taste carefully, adding more salt and pepper if the flavour is rather bland. Taste again after each addition until the sauce has a rich, deep flavour. Serve direct from the casserole or arrange on a serving dish with the sauce poured over. Garnish with chopped parsley.

• This rich dish is best accompanied by a purée of potatoes and some fresh greens.

M   Not suitable for microwave cookery

F   Freeze well-covered with sauce so that the meat doesn't dry out

AP Cook a day in advance and reheat when required

Roast duck with honey, lemon and mint sauce

Hwyaden gyda mel, lemon a mintys

This is a good way to serve duck. The freshness of the mint provides a lovely contrast to the richness of the duck, and the honey and lemon add a superb flavour. Of the forty or so varieties of mint found growing in Wales I favour apple mint for this dish, but lemon-, orange-, ginger- or spearmint would be almost as good.

1 tsp fresh mint, chopped
1 tsp honey
50 g (2 oz) butter
grated rind of 1 lemon
salt and freshly ground black
  pepper
1.8–2.25 k (4–5 lb) duck
50 ml (2 fl oz) water

For the sauce
2 tbsp lemon marmalade
2 tbsp water
2 tsp honey
juice of 1 large lemon
1 tbsp fresh mint, chopped

To garnish
lemon slices
a large sprig of fresh mint

1. Mix the mint with the honey, half of the butter, grated lemon rind and the seasoning. Place this mixture inside the duck. Rub the rest of the butter over the duck breast.
2. Put the duck in a roasting tin, pour the water around it and roast in a moderately hot oven (gas 6, 400°F, 200°C) for 1–1½ hours, basting frequently. To test if the duck is cooked pierce the fattest part of the leg with a skewer: if the juices run clear then the bird is cooked. Remove from the tin and keep warm.
3. For the sauce: gently heat the lemon marmalade in a sauce-pan with the water. Add the honey and the lemon juice

(don't add the cooking juices from the duck, they will be too fatty). Bring briefly to the boil. Add the chopped mint.
4. Garnish the duck with the lemon and fresh mint. Hand the sauce separately.

M   Suitable for microwave cookery. If possible prepare the sauce in the sauceboat to save extra work

F   Freeze the duck but not the sauce

AP   Prepare the duck up to the end of stage 1. Prepare the sauce in advance

Dark Age chicken
Cyw iar yr oesoedd tywyll

Imagine yourself back 1,400 years. The Romans with their luxurious lifestyle have fled our Isles and we are plunged back into the Iron Age. What could we find to feast on? Roger Worsley in his series 'Tastes of the Times' recommends this dish, known to the Celts as *Lay m wynias*, as a true Dark Age Recipe. Do try it, you won't believe how good it tastes.

100 ml (4 fl oz) dry white
    wine
1.35–1.6 k (3–3½ lb) roasting
    chicken
2 bay leaves

50 g (2 oz) fresh brown
    breadcrumbs
1 egg
salt and freshly ground black
    pepper

For the stuffing
100 g (4 oz) pine kernels (or
    almonds), finely chopped
100 g (4 oz) dates, finely
    chopped
25 g (1 oz) stem ginger,
    chopped (1 tbsp ginger
    preserve will do instead)

For the sauce
50 g (2 oz) pine kernels
25–50 g (1–2 oz) stem ginger
    (or 1 tbsp ginger preserve)
2 tsp wine vinegar
1 tbsp honey
¼ tsp cinnamon
¼ tsp mace
3 egg yolks

1. Pour the wine over the chicken and leave to soak overnight in the fridge.
2. Mix all the ingredients for the stuffing together and season to taste.
3. Drain the wine from the chicken and discard. Stuff the bird, tuck a bay leaf under each 'armpit' and roast in a moderate

oven (gas 4, 350°F, 180°C) for 1¼ hours or until cooked through.

4. Put all the ingredients for the sauce in a liquidizer and blend until smooth. Heat very gently in a saucepan, stirring all the time, and take off the heat as soon as it begins to thicken.

5. Serve the roast chicken cut into chunks or slices with the sauce handed separately.

• To complete your Dark Age meal serve the chicken with a salad, with cabbage cooked in ale or Croffta leeks (see p. 228).

M   Cook the chicken in the microwave and crisp under the grill to finish. It is safer to cook the sauce conventionally

F   Freeze the chicken but not the sauce

AP Prepare up to the end of stage 2

Venison pie
Pastai cig carw

Venison is now available throughout Wales from the small proportion of livestock farmers who have turned to this alternative animal husbandry. Farm venison is quite different from wild venison, and its milder flavour and softer texture suit many people today. Venison is the leanest of meat, with no wastage and a good gamey flavour. It is well suited to a crisp pastry coating and makes a suitable dish for a dinner party or family meal. My thanks to Caroline Clarke at Cefn Canol Deer Farm in Crymych Dyfed for this recipe.

50 g (2 oz) butter
675 g (1½ lb) haunch
  venison, diced
2 tbsp flour
salt and freshly ground black
  pepper
100 ml (4 fl oz) red wine
100 g (4 oz) mushrooms (field
  ones if possible), chopped
good bunch of fresh herbs,
  chopped

For the pastry
50 g (2 oz) butter
50 g (2 oz) lard – or use all
  butter if preferred
225 g (8 oz) plain flour
pinch of salt
water to bind
milk to glaze

1. Melt the butter in a heavy-based casserole and fry the venison a few cubes at a time to seal. Stir in the flour and seasoning and cook for another 3 minutes.
2. Add the wine, mushrooms and herbs, add water to cover, then cook in a slow oven (gas 1–2, 275–300°F, 140–150°C) until the meat is really tender, about 1½ hours.
3. Make up the pastry by rubbing the fats into the flour until the mixture resembles fine breadcrumbs, then adding the

salt and enough water to make a firm dough. Leave to rest for 30 minutes in the fridge.

4. Roll out the pastry into two rounds. Use one to line a deepish 25 cm (10 in) pie plate and spoon the cool, cooked venison on top. Cover with the remaining pastry and seal the edges with a little water, then press well together.

5. Brush with a little milk to glaze and bake the pie in a moderately hot oven (gas 5, 375°F, 190°C) for 20 minutes then lower the heat to gas 3 (325°F, 170°C) for a further 15 minutes to cook the pastry through underneath.

M   The venison may be cooked in the microwave

F   Freezes well

AP Cook the venison and make up the pastry in advance

Goose with apple stuffing

Gŵydd wedi'i stwffio gydag afal

In *First Catch Your Peacock* (1980) Bobby Freeman writes, 'Geese are still popular eating today in Wales, a reflection of their importance in early Welsh rural life. The *Laws of Hywel Dda* decreed that "the turbulent goose could be summarily executed" if found damaging standing corn, or corn in barns.'

Serves 8

5.4–6.3 k (12–14 lb) goose
25 g (1 oz) butter
4 tbsp red wine, Madeira or port blended with 4 tbsp water
8 rashers streaky bacon

For the stuffing
175 g (6 oz) wholemeal breadcrumbs
2 medium cooking apples or 1 large, peeled and finely chopped
1 medium onion, peeled and finely chopped
1 egg

salt and freshly ground black pepper
a handful of fresh sage leaves, chopped
1 tsp freshly grated nutmeg

For the apple sauce
1 large cooking apple, peeled and chopped
1 medium onion, chopped
25 g (1 oz) butter
100 ml (4 fl oz) cider
1 tsp honey
salt and freshly ground black pepper

1. Combine the ingredients for the stuffing. Stuff the breast cavity of the goose and secure with a skewer or thread. Spread the butter over the breast.
2. Put the bird in a large baking tin containing the wine, and roast in a slow oven (gas 3, 325°F, 170°C) for 20–25 minutes

to the pound, basting often. Lay the bacon across the breast for the last 30 minutes. To see if the goose is cooked, pierce the thickest part of the thigh with a skewer; if the juices run clear the goose is ready. Remove from the tin and keep warm.

3. For the apple sauce gently fry the apple and onion in the butter until soft. Add the cider and honey and season to taste. Serve the goose with the sauce handed separately.

M   Suitable for microwave cookery

F   Freeze the goose in joints or slices; freeze the sauce separately

AP Prepare the stuffing in advance, but don't stuff the goose until the time of roasting. Prepare the apple sauce ahead

Salt duck
Hwyaden hallt

'Salt boiled duck, with white onion sauce, is much better than roast duck,' wrote Lady Llanover in *Good Cookery* (1867). I have not tampered with her recipe for I feel that it reads well enough and should you have time and a duck on your hands then you will enjoy working directly under Lady Llanover's instruction. The duck is very tender and the salting removes any greasiness – really a clever way to deal with a duck, but remember to start preparations three days in advance.

Salt duck with onion sauce
For a common-sized duck a quarter of a pound of salt, to be well rubbed in and re-rubbed, and turned on a dish every day for three days then wash all the salt off clean, put it into a double* with half a pint of water to the pound, and let it simmer steadily for two hours.

Onion sauce
Cut up four onions and stew in a double with a little water until tender; then pour off the water and mix half an ounce of flour with it; then add half a pint of milk, and stir well until of a proper consistency, then pass through a wire sieve and return into the double saucepan; stir well, and when quite hot it is ready to pour over.

M   Not suitable for microwave cookery

F   Don't freeze the duck if it tastes extremely salty, since this will only be heightened through freezing

* A double as used by Lady Llanover is in fact a *bain-marie* (see p. 21).

AP Start 3 days ahead, complete the cooking of the duck and let it cool. Prepare the sauce and cool until required. Reheat the duck, well covered, in an ovenproof dish and put the sauce back in the double saucepan to reheat

Rabbit with damsons
Cwningen gydag eirin duon

First brought to our land by the Crusaders, the rabbit was treasured and closely guarded at first but eventually it became a real pest! We already had the native hare of course; anyone could have one of those for a meal, but the rabbit, or coney, was special. Only kings, princes and knights of the realm were allowed to partake of this luxury, and for a commoner to be caught eating coney was a hanging matter.

The main disadvantage with rabbit is that there are too many bones, but if cooked carefully the flesh will fall off the bone and the flavour is very good. Its firm flesh marries well with the sharpness of damsons. If they are unavailable, use plums or prunes and adjust the seasoning to taste.

1.35 k (3 lb) rabbit (preferably wild), jointed
1 dsp seasoned flour
1 tbsp olive oil
100 ml (4 fl oz) red wine
1 onion, sliced into rings
2 cloves garlic, crushed with salt
2 tsp fresh lovage (or substitute fresh chervil)
2 whole cloves
450 g (1 lb) damsons, stoned

To garnish
chopped parsley

1. Dip the rabbit joints in the seasoned flour and sauté in the oil until golden brown on all sides. Remove the rabbit, add the wine to the pan and boil up well.
2. In a heavy-based casserole arrange the onion, garlic, lovage and cloves and put the rabbit joints on top. Add the wine and pan-juices and the damsons, then cover and cook in a warm oven (gas 3, 325°F, 170°C) for 1½ hours or until the rabbit is really tender.

3. Serve direct from the casserole, garnished with chopped parsley.

● The richness of this dish requires little more accompaniment than a bowl of creamed potatoes or plain boiled brown rice and perhaps a crisp green vegetable.

M   Suitable for microwave cookery

F   Freezes well, thaw completely before reheating

AP Prepare and cook the day before. Reheat gently when required

Welsh chicken pie
Pastai cyw iar cymreig

Once a luxury, chicken is now common to all dining tables, but alas, today's frozen birds need special cooking to give them any flavour at all. This recipe suits any chicken, but particularly an old hen such as those scratching round a Welsh farmyard, full of flavour but perhaps a bit on the tough side.

1.35 k (3 lb) chicken
1 carrot
¼ onion
1 stick celery
bunch of fresh herbs or dried *bouquet garni*
50 g (2 oz) butter or hard margarine
100 g (4 oz) lean smoked bacon, diced
2 medium leeks, sliced
2 tbsp flour
salt and freshly ground black pepper
2 tbsp fresh parsley, chopped

For the rough puff pastry (or use 400 g (14 oz) bought puff pastry)
225 g (8 oz) flour
pinch of salt
175 g (6 oz) butter or firm margarine
150 ml (¾ pint) iced water
1 egg yolk mixed with 1 tsp water to glaze

1. Remove the giblets and put them together with the chicken in a large saucepan. Add the carrot, onion, celery and *bouquet garni* and enough water to cover.
2. Bring to the boil then simmer very gently for 1¼ hours or until the chicken is cooked. To test, pull off a leg and if there is any sign of blood at the joint, continue cooking. Once cooked, leave the bird to cool in the liquid.
3. Melt the butter and fry the bacon and leeks gently for 10

minutes. Stir in the flour, cook for a further 2 minutes then add 600 ml (1 pint) of the liquid, strained, in which the chicken was poached. Bring to the boil, stirring all the time, season to taste and add the parsley.

4. Cut the flesh off the chicken and mix into the sauce, then pour into a 1.2 l (2 pint) pie dish and cool.

5. Make up the pastry as on p. 119 and roll out. Damp the lip of the pie dish and press a strip of pastry on to it. Then damp the pastry strip and press the pastry lid on to this to secure it. Trim the edges.

6. Brush the top of the pie with the egg wash, decorate it with any pastry trimmings. Bake for 30 minutes in a hot oven (gas 7, 425°F, 220°C) then turn the heat down to gas 5 (375°F, 190°C) and cook for a further 10 minutes.

• Serve with punchnep (see p.000) and some crisp broccoli.

M   Not suitable for microwave cookery

F   Freezes well. Thaw completely before reheating

AP Prepare up to the end of stage 4 and make the pastry

MEAT

Steak and kidney cobbler
Pork St Tudno
Beef, mushroom and herb pie
Bacon and leek pudding
Beef in Welsh beer
Faggots
Ham Pencarreg
Harvest hot pot
Kidneys Ceredigion
Fillets of lamb stuffed with spinach and
    brown bread
Lamb and laverbread roll
Rack of Welsh lamb with a honey, garlic and
    white wine sauce
Lamburgers
Lamb and mint sausages
Pickled pork
Pan-fried pork with wild garlic
Spareribs in honey
Welsh lamb chops with sweet herbs
Roast leg of lamb with ginger, honey, cider
    and rosemary
Beef and ham loaf
Katt pie
Loin of pork Llandeilo
Rack of lamb with lavender

'The leg of mutton of Wales beats the leg of mutton of any other country, and I had never tasted a Welsh leg of mutton before. Certainly I shall never forget the first Welsh leg of mutton which I tasted, rich but delicate, replete with juices derived from the aromatic herbs of the noble Berwyn, cooked to a turn and weighing just four pounds.' George Borrow in *Wild Wales* (1862).

But why should Welsh lamb taste different? Is it the breed or the feed, or perhaps the environment in which it is reared? A combination of all three must be the answer. Welsh mountain sheep are a stocky breed, lean but hardy, and well able to cope with life on an unfriendly, cold, windy and often very wet mountain in remote parts of Wales. Grazing is often scarce and these tough little sheep are used to foraging for their diet. Of course, food is brought up from the farm and the sheep are well cared for, but in the winter there are no lush green valley pastures for them to enjoy.

Why bother to eat lamb in March when the flavour can be no more mature than the beast? Born prematurely, they are reared inside and fed to be fat enough for the table by Easter. No, it is better to wait until the end of the summer when the mountain lambs appear in the butchers'. They are born naturally with the onset of the spring weather, have nibbled their way over the summer pastures, and their tender flesh will have a depth of flavour and very little fat. Thus the quality of the much-praised Welsh lamb can be attributed to its slow maturing over a longer period on natural foodstuffs.

Pigs are the natural companions to any rural community. Needing little looking after, they eat anything and everything. Once slaughtered, a pig will provide enough meat to feed a family for many months, starting with faggots made from the offal, and of course blood pudding, then fresh cuts of meat, brawn, and all the salted, cured, pickled and smoked cuts and joints which can be stored for the future.

Pigs and sheep are still commonly reared in Wales but the large cattle herds with which the early Celts measured their wealth are sadly depleted. Lady Llanover, writing in 1867, mentions the Pembroke or Castle Martin breed as admirable for beef and excellent milkers. She goes on to say, 'The old Pembroke breed, white with black ears, and remarkably handsome, are becoming extinct, and those that remain are wild from want of care. The Glamorgan cows are magnificent animals, black, with a white stripe down the tail, excellent milkers. The Carmarthen cattle are black, very much like the Pembroke, also good for milk. In the counties of Brecon and Radnor, the landowners have generally introduced Herefords and Shorthorns, which are inferior in many respects to various breeds of Welsh cattle. Merioneth has a small breed which, if well kept, would prove valuable.'

Meat, though, is not considered vital to the diet now as it once was. Some people eat none at all whilst most of us eat far less than we used to. Fish, vegetables and pulses are taking the place of meat and, of course, in many respects provide a healthier alternative. If we eat less meat then should we not be more choosy over what we buy and enjoy every bite? Fat is a forbidden word these days, but don't become too puritanical, for a little fat marbled into the fine grain of a beef steak will not only make it tender but stop it drying out during cooking.

Look out for alternative cuts and cooking methods. Stews, so much part of the Celtic kitchen when the large pot suspended over the open fire was the only method of cooking, are still the ideal way to cook the tougher cuts of meat. By immersing meat in a well-flavoured sauce you not only make it more tender but also add flavour. Basic stew at one end of the scale leads up to beef in red wine at the other.

Grilling is a healthy method of cooking meat, but beware, the shorter the cooking time the better quality the meat must be. Go for the best and buy lean, top-quality cuts. If you spend a small fortune on your meat then don't drown the flavour in thick and powerful sauces, just add the merest suggestion of seasoning and perhaps a knob of herb butter.

Lastly, don't forget offal. Tender and tasty whether you casserole or sauté it, this cheap form of meat is less fatty than most.

Enjoy your meat, get to know your butcher and stick with him. Take time and care over the preparation and cooking: if you eat less, then make sure it's the best.

Steak and kidney cobbler
Pastai cig eidion ac arennau

This conjures up memories of my childhood, and steaming hot family lunches on a Saturday. More often than not my mother would prepare and cook the meat on Friday and then reheat it with the scone topping late on Saturday morning. It filled the house with mouthwatering aromas just as we arrived home after running our various errands, and whatever our appetites, all were satisfied after mother's steak and kidney cobbler. You may adjust this dish to suit your purse and palate; simply prepare a casserole of whatever meat you prefer and cook in the same way with the scone topping.

675 g (1½ lb) stewing steak or
  similar
225 g (½ lb) ox kidney
seasoned flour
1 small onion, finely chopped
1 tbsp parsley, chopped
stock or water to cover

For the scone topping
225 g (8 oz) self-raising flour
pinch of salt
1 tsp dried thyme or
  marjoram
5 g (2 oz) butter or margarine
100 ml (¼ pint) milk

1. Cut the steak and kidney into 1.5 cm (½ in) cubes, discarding all fat and sinew. Roll them in the seasoned flour until well coated.
2. Put the meat into a 1.2–1.7 l (2–3 pint) casserole with a well-fitting lid. Scatter the onion and parsley over and add enough brown stock (a cube will do) or water to cover the meat. Cover and cook in a slow oven (gas 3, 325°F, 170°C) for about 1½ hours or until the meat is very tender.
3. To make the scone topping: sift the flour into a large bowl. Stir in the salt and herbs and rub in the butter until the mixture resembles fine breadcrumbs. Pour in the milk and

stir the dough quickly with a palette knife. With well-floured hands quickly shape the dough into small buns about 5 cm (2 in) across, or use a pastry cutter.

4. Turn the oven up to gas 7 (425°F, 220°C). Taste the meat and adjust the seasoning. Then arrange the scones on top of the meat so that they sit in the juices. Put the casserole immediately back in the hot oven, uncovered.

5. The scone topping should take no more than 15 minutes to rise up, cook through and turn a golden brown, but this will depend on how hot the casserole was when the scone dough was put in. Serve straight out of the oven with some fresh vegetables.

M   Adapts well to microwave cookery

F   Cook the scones and meat together but freeze separately

AP Prepare and cook the meat, keep overnight in the fridge. Make up and cook the scone topping when required

Pork St Tudno
Porc San Tudno

Anyone visiting Llandudno in North Wales will have found reference to St Tudno. He was the son of Seithenin Frenin, King of Maes Gwyddno or 'Plain' of Gwyddno, which was overwhelmed by water in the 6th century and now forms the bed of Cardigan Bay.

I'm sure St Tudno would have enjoyed this delicately flavoured dish of pork with apples. It is extremely quick to prepare and healthy, too, without any added thickeners, for the apples add a natural tang and moisture to the pork while it cooks.

4 thick pork chops
salt and freshly ground black
  pepper
½ tsp fresh ginger, grated
1 tsp honey
3–4 large cooking apples,
  peeled, cored and thinly
  sliced

juice of ½ lemon
1 tbsp soft brown sugar
50 g (2 oz) unsalted butter,
  melted

To garnish
chopped parsley
lemon twists

1. Trim any excess fat from the chops and put them in a single layer into a buttered ovenproof dish. Season well with salt and pepper, add the ginger and honey and arrange the apple over the chops.
2. Squeeze over the lemon juice, add the sugar and pour over half the melted butter. Cover with a lid or some foil and bake in a warm oven (gas 3, 325°F, 170°C) for 1 hour.
3. Remove the lid, brush the apples with the remaining butter and bake uncovered for a further 10 minutes or until the apples are golden brown and the pork chops tender. Serve garnished with the parsley and lemon twists.

- Baked jacket potatoes and punchnep (see p. 202) go well with this dish.

M   Not suitable for microwave cookery

F   Freeze in the cooking dish so that the chops needn't be disturbed during thawing and reheating

AP Prepare up to the end of stage 2. To reheat, continue with stage 3 but cook for a further 20 minutes until the apples are golden brown and the chops hot right through

Beef, mushroom and herb pie

Pastai cig eidion, madarch a pherlysiau

'The hermit selected a small sprig of orange thyme, a little savory and basil, twisting them together with a bit of thread, and then stirred the fragrant nosegay round two or three times, till it had imparted sufficient flavour to the sauce.' Lady Llanover's *Good Cookery* (1867).

This pie has a rich beef filling and is surrounded with a savoury choux pastry. Do have a go at the pastry; it's straightforward to prepare and spectacular to serve, and I'm sure you'll find the end result rewarding.

675 g (1½ lb) rump steak,
  cubed
seasoned flour
3 tbsp sunflower oil
225 g (8 oz) onions, sliced
175 g (6 oz) mushrooms,
  sliced
½ bottle red wine
handful of fresh herbs tied, or
  a dried *bouquet garni*
salt and freshly ground black
  pepper

For the choux pastry
75 g (3 oz) butter
225 ml (8 fl oz) water
100 g (4 oz) flour, sifted
pinch of salt
1 tsp dry English mustard
1 tsp parsley, finely chopped
3 eggs

1. Coat the steak in the seasoned flour. In a large, heavy-based casserole heat the oil and fry the beef, a few cubes at a time, until brown on all sides.
2. Remove the beef and fry the onions gently for 5 minutes until soft, adding more oil if necessary. Toss in the mushrooms and fry for another 2 minutes, until all the oil is absorbed.
3. Return the beef to the casserole, pour in the wine, and

enough water to cover, add the herbs and seasoning and cover with a lid. Put in a warm oven (gas 3, 325°F, 170°C) for an hour. Cool.

4. For the pastry: cut the butter into cubes and put in a saucepan with the water. Bring slowly to the boil, making sure that all the butter has melted before the water even begins to simmer. Turn the heat up, let the water come to a rousing boil and tip in the sifted flour, salt, mustard and parsley all at once. Remove from the heat and beat quickly with a wooden spoon until smooth and shiny. Let the dough cool, then add the eggs one by one, beating hard between each addition. The pastry can now be left covered until ready to cook the pie.

5. With a spatula or palette knife spread the pastry around the sides of a large, shallow ovenproof dish. Put the cold beef and mushroom mixture into the middle and bake in the centre of a moderately hot oven (gas 6, 400°F, 200°C) for 30–40 minutes, or until the pastry is really crisp, brown and well puffed up around the aromatic beef filling. Serve immediately.

• Heatproof soup bowls can be lined with the pastry and served as individual pies if you prefer.

M The beef may be microwaved but the pastry must be cooked conventionally

F The filling may be frozen but not the pastry

AP Prepare the beef a day or so in advance. The pastry can be made up a few hours in advance and then spread around the pie dish and cooked when required

Bacon and leek pudding
Pwdin cig moch a chennin

'Wise men informed me that bacon from a pig slaughtered when the moon was "on her weakness" would not cure properly and would be heir to most of the consequent blemishes, rancidity, slime and even worse!' James Williams in *Give Me Yesterday*.

There is nothing more satisfying on a cold winter's day than a filling steamed pudding. It is simple to make, especially in a microwave, and now that vegetable suet is easily obtainable it is a wholesome and nutritious dish.

For the wholemeal suet crust
225 g (8 oz) self-raising wholemeal flour
100 g (4 oz) shredded suet (animal or vegetable)
50 g (2 oz) fresh brown breadcrumbs
salt to taste
cold water to mix

For the filling
12 rashers of lean, de-rinded bacon
3 medium leeks, well washed
freshly ground black pepper
1 tbsp winter savory, chopped (or substitute thyme)
chicken stock
a little butter

1. To make the pastry, combine the flour, suet, breadcrumbs and salt in a large bowl. Add enough cold water to make a firm dough and mix well. Turn out on to a floured board and knead for about a minute then divide the pastry into two, one piece twice the size of the other. Roll the larger piece of dough out to 1.5 cm (½ in) thickness and use to line a well-buttered 1.2 l (2 pint) pudding basin. Reserve the remaining pastry for the lid.
2. For the filling, cut each leek into four and roll each piece in a

rasher of bacon. Pack these into the pudding basin, pressing them well down, and sprinkle each layer with pepper and winter savory. Add enough chicken stock to come three-quarters of the way up the bacon and leeks.

3. Roll the remaining pastry out to form a lid. Cover the pudding, dampen the pastry edges and press them firmly together.

4. Cover the basin with buttered greaseproof paper, pleated in the centre, and a layer of pleated foil on top (the pleat allows the pudding to expand).

5. Place in a saucepan containing enough boiling water to come halfway up the basin and cover with a tightly closed lid, or put in a steamer, and steam for 3 hours, taking care to top up with boiling water occasionally. Serve direct from the bowl.

M Steamed puddings work superbly in the microwave. Do not use foil, but cover the pudding with a sheet of damp greaseproof paper, secured with an elastic band, to prevent the suet crust from drying out on top. Adjust timings to suit your microwave power, but I suggest about 10 minutes on a medium setting

F Freeze a portion if leftover, but I don't recommend it for the whole pudding

AP Alas, the pastry is not nearly as good if made in advance, as it will not rise enough when cooked

Beef in Welsh beer
Cig eidion mewn cwrw Cymreig

This recipe was given to me by Felinfoel Brewery, a small traditional brewery situated in the village of Felinfoel on the outskirts of Llanelli. Founded in 1840 by David John, a local iron and tinplate master, the present brewery was built in 1878 in the grounds of his home, the bottling store being erected on the old tennis court. The company distributes its beers through seventy-five public houses in Dyfed, where no doubt some landlords will also serve you this fine beef casserole to accompany your pint.

675 g (1½ lb) lean braising
  beef
50 g (2 oz) dripping
225 g (8 oz) onions, sliced
2 tbsp flour
12 g (½ oz) caster sugar
salt and freshly ground black
  pepper

1 tbsp fresh oregano or
  marjoram, or 1 tsp dried
660 ml (1 pint) homemade
  brown stock (or use a stock
  cube)
600 ml (1 pint) pale ale

1. Cut the meat into 4 cm (1½ in) cubes. Melt the dripping in a heavy-based casserole and fry the meat, a few cubes at a time, until brown on all sides.
2. Remove the meat and fry the onions in the dripping until soft. Stir in the flour and cook for 2 minutes, then add the sugar, seasoning, herbs, stock and beer and bring to the boil.
3. Return the meat to the casserole, cover with a tight-fitting lid and simmer gently in a moderate oven (gas 4, 350°F, 180°C) till the meat is tender, about 2 hours. Adjust seasoning to taste.

- Serve with fresh vegetables and boiled Pembrokeshire potatoes.

M   Suitable for microwave cookery

F   Freeze well covered, thaw completely before reheating to stop the meat breaking up

AP Cook the day before and reheat gently when required

Faggots

Ffagots

Called *crépinettes* in France, these balls of offal are wrapped in the pig's caul, or apron, which moistens them during cooking, adding extra flavour as well. In Wales it is traditional to include the pig's fry in faggots; these are the lights, liver and melts (heart), and they give Welsh faggots their special flavour. Faggots are the staple diet of Welsh rugby players, or so I am told, and are served almost always at the end of the game to feed both the home and away teams.

Makes 18–24

450 g (1 lb) pig's fry (lights, liver and heart) – or use all liver

piece of pig's caul or apron (optional)

1 medium onion

100 g (4 oz) brown breadcrumbs

1 tsp salt

1 tsp freshly ground black pepper

1 tsp fresh winter savory (or substitute sage)

1. Soak the pig's caul in tepid water for 30 minutes.
2. In a saucepan, cover the lights, liver and heart with cold water and bring to the boil, simmer for 15 minutes.
3. Mince or process the liver, lights, heart and onion. Add the breadcrumbs, seasoning and sage.
4. Cut the caul into 10 cm (4 in) squares and put 2 tbsp mixture on each piece; fold and roll into balls. If you aren't using caul, simply wet your hands and roll the mixture into balls.
5. Place in a greased baking tin and bake for 30 minutes in a hot oven (gas 7, 425°F, 220°C) until the faggots are well browned on top and the juices run clear when pierced with a fork.

- Traditionally served hot with peas and a good rich gravy.

M   Not suitable for microwave cookery

F   Freeze individually, well wrapped

AP Make in advance, chill until required. Reheat, covered, in a
    medium oven (gas 4, 350°F, 180°C) for 30 minutes or in a
    microwave

Ham Pencarreg

Pencarreg cheese has been carefully developed over the past few years to become the first Brie-type cheese made in Wales. It has an individual flavour and ripening texture. Dougal Campbell takes infinite care in his small cheese factory in Lampeter to ensure that only organically produced milk is used and the very highest hygiene standards maintained to produce this special cheese.

Llanboidy is another characteristic cheese from Dyfed. Made with the milk from a rare breed of cows known as Red Poll, it is the most flavoursome of farmhouse cheeses.

By making use of local products Barry Headland, at the Fourcroft Hotel in Tenby, has created this simple but delicious dish which is much enjoyed by his clientele. To re-create the same flavours you must choose carefully from alternative products and I suggest you substitute a well-flavoured farmhouse Brie for Pencarreg and a mature farmhouse Cheddar for Llanboidy, if necessary.

8 thin slices home-cured ham
8 sticks celery, taken from the middle
100 g (4 oz) Pencarreg cheese

For the cheese sauce
50 g (2 oz) butter

50 g (2 oz) flour
600 ml (1 pint) milk
100 g (4 oz) Llanboidy cheese, grated
salt and freshly ground black pepper

1. Wrap each slice of ham around a stick of celery and a sliver of Pencarreg. Lay the ham rolls in a greased ovenproof dish.
2. For the sauce, melt the butter gently in a saucepan, stir in the flour and cook for a minute, then gradually pour in the

Mussel pâté with Melba toast

Scallops in gin

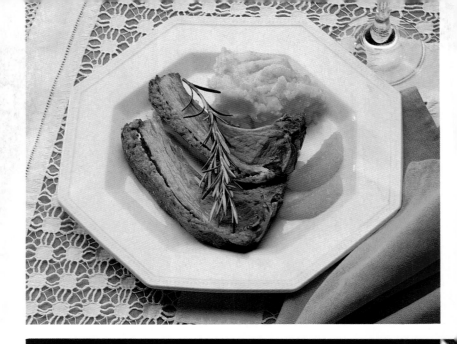

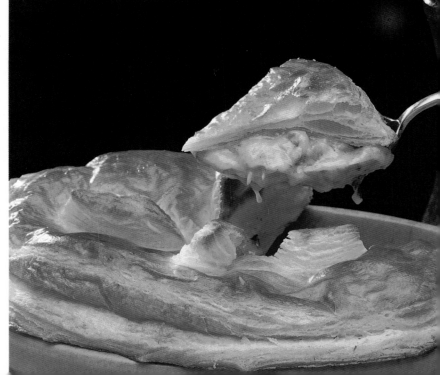

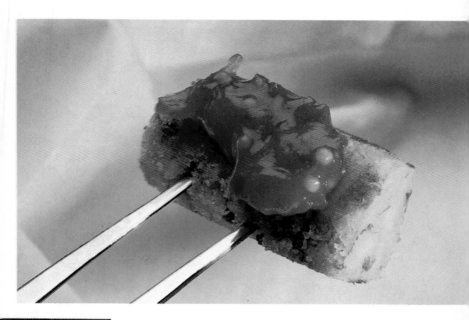

ABOVE LEFT

*Rack of lamb with lavender
and punchnep*

ABOVE RIGHT

*Glamorgan sausage with
tomato pickle*

LEFT

Welsh chicken pie

Honey and ginger syllabub, blackcurrant layer pudding

Home preserves

ABOVE LEFT

Welsh baking: pikelets, Bara Brith, wholemeal bread, scones and Welsh cakes

ABOVE

Baking on a bakestone over an open hearth

LEFT

Ingredients for a miner's lunch box

Farmhouse cheese coming out of the press

Cockle-gathering ladies returning from the sands

milk. Stir continuously as you bring the sauce up to the boil.
Add the grated cheese and season to taste.

3. Pour the sauce over the ham rolls and bake in a hot oven
   (gas 7, 425°F, 220°C) for 20 minutes until bubbling and golden
   brown on top.

M   Cook in the microwave. Brown under a grill to finish

F   Not advisable, the crunch will be lost from the celery

AP Assemble the entire dish in advance, but cool the sauce
    completely before pouring over the ham. Reheat when
    required

Harvest hot pot
Cawl diolchgarwch

Imagine yourself as a potato picker a hundred years ago in Wales, returning from the fields, weary and aching, to be welcomed by a hot meal all ready for the table. This hot pot would have been prepared early in the day and left hanging in a large cauldron over the open fire to cook through. Simple but nourishing.

25 g (1 oz) butter
225 g (8 oz) lean smoked
   bacon, cut into pieces
225 g (8 oz) lean lamb, cubed
450 g (1 lb) potatoes, peeled
   and cubed
450 g (1 lb) carrots, cubed
4 good-sized leeks, chopped

225 g (8 oz) swede or turnip,
   chopped
handful of mixed fresh herbs,
   chopped
salt and freshly ground black
   pepper
1.2 l (2 pints) water

1. In a large, heavy-based casserole melt the butter and fry the meat to brown it on all sides.
2. Add all the prepared vegetables, herbs, seasonings and water, cover the pot and simmer gently for 1¾ hours.
• Serve with chunks of fresh wholemeal bread and butter or slices of cheese and apple potato cake (see p. 203).

M   An ideal dish for the microwave from stage 2.

F   Freezes well, but thaw completely before reheating to prevent the vegetables breaking up

AP Cook a day in advance. Chill overnight in the fridge and reheat very gently in a warm oven (gas 3, 325°F, 170°C) until piping hot

Kidneys Ceredigion

Arennau Ceredigion

Stay in a farmhouse in the Ceredigion region of Wales and you'll find that it offers superb value. Not only do you get top-quality comfort, a working farm to explore, and the company of the farmer's family, but also food worthy of medals for its quality and quantity. During the winter months farmers' wives experiment with recipes using produce from the farm so that once the summer season starts they can offer an extended menu to their visitors.

14 lamb's kidneys
seasoned flour
100 g (4 oz) butter
salt and freshly ground black
   pepper

6 tbsp red wine or stock
2 tbsp Dijon mustard
squeeze of lemon juice

To garnish
chopped parsley

1. Skin, halve and core each kidney and slice into about three pieces. Toss in the seasoned flour.
2. Heat 75 g (3 oz) of the butter in a large frying pan and quickly sauté the kidneys until they are just firm and lightly browned. (Do them in batches if you haven't got a large pan.)
3. Season, add the wine or stock, reduce the heat and simmer very gently for 2–3 minutes, then add the mustard and a good squeeze of lemon juice.
4. Take the pan off the heat and stir in the remaining butter cut into slivers. Garnish with the parsley.
- Serve with some nutty brown rice (see p. 134) or perhaps an onion cake (see p. 221).

M   Not advisable, the kidneys will stew rather than fry briskly

F   Not suitable for freezing

AP Prepare stage 1

Fillets of lamb stuffed with spinach and brown bread

Tafellau cig oen wedi'u stwffio gyda phigoglys a bara brown

Earlier this century white bread was what the Welsh wanted to eat, and so the bakers complied. Nowadays, like our health-conscious neighbours throughout the United Kingdom we all choose brown. From his renovated water mill Felin Geri at Cwm Cou, Michael Heycock supplies stoneground flour to a huge proportion of his neighbours for making into wholemeal bread. He gave me the idea for this recipe, and a better taste from more natural ingredients you couldn't wish to find.

675–900 g (1½–2 lb) neck fillets of lamb

450 g (1 lb) fresh spinach, blanched and chopped

100 g (4 oz) wholemeal breadcrumbs

1 medium onion, finely chopped

1 clove of garlic, crushed with salt

1 tbsp fresh marjoram, chopped

50 g (2 oz) butter

100 ml (4 fl oz) white wine

1. Trim the lamb fillets of all fat and sinew. Bat them flat with a heavy instrument; a wooden mallet is good or just a sturdy wooden spoon.
2. Arrange the fillets side by side on a chopping board and spread the chopped spinach, breadcrumbs, onion, garlic and marjoram over the surface. Roll the fillets up into one long sausage and tie in several places to secure.
3. Melt the butter in a large roasting tin and when it begins to sizzle put in the lamb and pour the wine round. Roast in a hot oven (gas 7, 425°F, 220°C) for 20 minutes, turning once or twice so that all sides of the lamb brown.

4. Arrange the lamb, string removed, on a large dish and cut into slices. Stir the pan juices and pour over the lamb just before serving.

• A vegetable dish of, say, broad beans in sour cream (see p. 220) or pumpkin in cheese sauce (see p. 230) would marry well with this, and can be prepared ahead of time to be reheated while the lamb is in the oven.

M   Not suitable for microwave cookery

F   Not suitable for freezing

AP Prepare up to the end of stage 2

Lamb and laverbread roll

Rholyn cig oen a bara lawr

If you ever need to serve a celebration meal on St David's Day (1 March) this is a real party piece for Welsh guests. Lamb and laverbread go surprisingly well together and the grated orange rind complements them both. Substitute chopped spinach and a little finely chopped anchovy if you are unable to buy laverbread; this will fool your guests, if you can keep the secret!

By rolling the loin of lamb in breadcrumbs a crisp outer shell is created to absorb the fat and I find that even the most ardent 'fat haters' will enjoy lamb served this way.

675–900 g (1½–2 lb) loin of lamb, skinned and boned (see p. 18, or ask your butcher to do it)
seasoned flour
1 egg, beaten
fresh brown breadcrumbs
50 g (2 oz) lard

For the stuffing
1 rasher streaky bacon, chopped
1 medium onion, chopped
50 g (2 oz) laverbread
grated rind of ½ orange

salt and freshly ground black pepper

For the sauce
25 g (1 oz) butter
1 small onion, finely diced
1 tbsp flour
300 ml (½ pint) good brown stock
1 tsp tomato purée
juice of ½ orange
3 tbsp red wine
salt and freshly ground black pepper

1. To make the stuffing, dry fry the bacon gently in a pan until the fat runs, add the onion and cook for a further 5 minutes until soft but not brown. Add the laverbread, grated orange rind and seasoning. Leave to cool.
2. Spread the stuffing down the centre of the loin, roll it up and

with a strong thread, sew loosely (so that the meat can expand during cooking) to form a long sausage shape.

3. Roll the loin in seasoned flour then brush with beaten egg and roll in the breadcrumbs, pressing them on with a palette knife so that the entire loin is covered.

4. In a moderately hot oven (gas 6, 400°F, 200°C) melt the dripping in a roasting pan and roast the loin for 1 hour, turning every 15 minutes so that it browns evenly on all sides.

5. Meanwhile, make the sauce: melt the butter and cook the onion over very gentle heat for 10 minutes. Stir in the flour and continue to cook gently until the flour has turned a good mid-brown colour. Gradually add the stock, tomato purée, orange juice and red wine. Season well and leave to simmer for 20 minutes. Strain and adjust seasoning before serving.

6. Leave the cooked loin to rest for 5 minutes, then carefully pull out the thread. Serve the loin of lamb carved into slices with the sauce passed separately.

M　Not suitable for microwave cookery

F　Freeze the lamb whole or in slices, well covered. Freeze sauce separately

AP　Prepare up to the end of stage 3. Prepare the sauce in advance

Rack of Welsh lamb with a honey, garlic and white wine sauce

Cig oen cymreig gyda saws mel, garlleg a gwin gwyn

'The woman next door was very civil, and gave me a shoulder of lamb, with a lesson in cooking, as though I had watched my mother for more than two years for nothing.' Richard Llewellyn, *How Green Was My Valley*.

Yes, the Welsh know how to cook lamb, a meat that is readily adaptable to any form of cooking. The cheaper cuts are often the tastiest and this sauce of honey, garlic and white wine will go well with any cut; you could substitute a leg, shoulder, breast or even chops.

675–900 g (1½–2 lb) best end of neck of lamb, skinned and chined (see p. 18, or ask your butcher to do it)
2 cloves garlic, crushed with salt

2 tbsp honey
150 ml (¼ pint) dry white wine
salt and freshly ground black pepper
1 tsp fresh rosemary

1. Score the thin layer of fat covering the lamb into a diamond pattern. Combine the crushed garlic, honey, wine, seasoning and rosemary and marinade the meat in this mixture for 30 minutes.
2. Sit the lamb on a wire rack above a roasting tin. Pour the juices from the marinade over the meat and let them drip through into the pan below. Roast in a hot oven (gas 7, 425°F, 220°C) for 30 minutes, or a little longer if you don't like your lamb pink.
3. Serve the lamb cut down between the rib bones either as single cutlets or doubles, or simply cut the meat off the rib cage and serve in slices.

4. The juices in the bottom of the pan can be served spooned over the meat just as they are. But if you prefer a thick gravy, add 1 tsp arrowroot mixed with 1 tbsp cold water or some kneaded butter (see p. 20) to the juices and let them boil up well.

- A rack of lamb served like this needs to be eaten at once, and I suggest that you prepare a dish of vegetables that can be pulled from the oven just as the lamb is ready. Say, a leek and potato pie (see p. 222) that could cook on the shelf below the lamb, or an onion cake (see p. 221).

M   Not suitable for microwave cookery

F   Not suitable for freezing

AP Make up the marinade and leave the lamb in it overnight. Don't roast the lamb ahead of time though

Lamburgers
Byrgars cig oen

Why stick to hamburgers when you can bite into twice the flavour with a lamburger? Ideal for barbecues, lamb is full of moisture and its flavour is improved with quick cooking over hot charcoal.

450 g (1 lb) lean lamb, shoulder or leg
2 tbsp coarse oatmeal
1 clove garlic, crushed with salt

4 fresh mint leaves, finely chopped
salt and freshly ground black pepper
4 soft wholemeal baps, sliced

1. In a food processor or similar, mince the lamb until fairly fine.
2. Combine the meat with the oatmeal, crushed garlic, chopped mint and seasoning to taste. Shape into 4 round 'cakes'.
3. Either barbecue over hot coals for about 4 minutes each side, or pan-fry or grill them.
4. Fill each bap with a burger and eat at once.

M   Not suitable for microwave cookery

F   Don't freeze for more than a week

AP Make up the burgers; cook when required

Lamb and mint sausages

Cig oen a mintys selsig

These are a great favourite with the Welsh. Many butchers now make lamb and mint sausages to their own recipes and children seem particularly fond of them. Ideal family food, simple to make and cook, and so much healthier than commercial sausages.

450 g (1 lb) shoulder of lamb
   or similar
1 medium onion
4 slices white bread, crusts
   removed, made into
   breadcrumbs

1 egg
4 leaves fresh mint, chopped,
   or 1 tsp dried mint
salt and freshly ground black
   pepper
fat for frying

1. In a food processor or similar, finely mince the lamb and onion. Add the breadcrumbs, egg, mint and lots of seasoning and mix well. *Do taste the mixture to check the seasoning.*
2. Shape the mixture into 8–12 sausages, roll on a floured board then fry gently in hot fat for about 10 minutes to cook through. If grilling, brush the sausages with a little oil beforehand. Without skins these sausages may break up on a barbecue, but you could wrap them in a rasher of streaky bacon and secure them with a cocktail stick.

M   Not suitable for microwave cookery

F   Not suitable for freezing

AP Make up the sausages; cook when required

Pickled pork

Porc wedi'i biclo

'I can remember the day that the butcher came to slaughter the pig. All our friends and neighbours gathered round and he hung the dead pig in the garage. Then my mother took the warm blood to make blood pudding but it was my aunt who always made the faggots. Before he left the butcher would remove the bladder and blow it up like a football, then throw it at the youngest child there. It was his bit of fun. Over the next few weeks my father would salt the various bits of pork, some we gave to neighbours and others we hung in the chimney to be cured for next winter.' This vivid account was given to me by Mrs Davies from Carmarthen.

1 hand and spring pork	300 ml (½ pint) pale ale
175 g (6 oz) coarse salt	300 ml (½ pint) stout
12 g (½ oz) saltpetre	1 bay leaf

1. To pickle: trim the pork and remove trotter if still attached. Rub salt into the surface of the joint and put into a dish.
2. Dissolve salt and saltpetre in a pan with the pale ale and stout. Bring to the boil, stirring occasionally, then pour over the joint and add the bay leaf. Cover and leave in a cool place, turning daily, for one week.
3. To cook the pork: remove from the liquid and put in a roasting tin. Cover with foil and bake in a moderately hot oven (gas 5, 375°F, 190°C) for 25 minutes per lb plus 25 minutes.
4. Remove from the tin and peel off the skin. Serve hot, surrounded by a selection of fresh vegetables, or leave to cool and serve with chutney.

M   Suitable for microwave cookery

F   Freeze in slices for easy thawing

AP Think ahead!

Pan-fried pork with wild garlic
Porc gyda garlleg gwyllt

Ramsons, or wild garlic, grow in great profusion in Wales. The pungent smell can be almost overpowering in spring and early summer, as you will find out should you wander through the dense woods which surround Castle Coch just to the north of Cardiff. Although the aroma is strong, the flavour of chopped garlic leaves is surprisingly gentle and they need very little cooking. So either add a handful of raw chopped ramsons to your salads or, as in this recipe, cook at the very last minute to preserve the flavour and texture.

1 clove garlic
600 ml (20 fl oz) single cream
675–900 g (1½–2 lb) fillet of
  pork
1 tbsp olive oil
25 g (1 oz) butter
salt and freshly ground black
  pepper

75 ml (3 fl oz) white wine
4 fresh wild garlic leaves,
  chopped (or substitute
  1 tbsp chopped chives)

To garnish
wild garlic leaves, or chopped
  chives

1. First make the sauce. Crush the clove of garlic with a little salt until it becomes almost a paste, add to the cream in a saucepan and bring to the boil. Simmer for at least 15 minutes until the cream has reduced by almost half and is of a thick consistency.
2. Meanwhile, trim the pork fillets of all skin, fat and sinew. Cut on the slant into 2.5 cm (1 in) wide slices, and bat out with a wooden spoon.
3. In a large, heavy-based frying pan, heat the oil and butter. Season the pork slices then fry quickly on both sides to seal. Add the wine before lowering the heat to medium to cook

the pork through. This should take no longer than 5 minutes in all.

4. Dish up the pork, add seasoning and the chopped wild garlic leaves to the sauce and pour immediately over the meat. Serve without delay, garnished with finely chopped garlic leaves or chopped chives and a colourful vegetable dish such as parsnip pie (see p. 205).

M   Not suitable for microwave cookery

F   Not suitable for freezing

AP   Make the sauce in advance. Cover with clingfilm, pressed well down on to the surface of the sauce to stop a skin forming, then reheat when required. Slice the raw pork fillet

Spareribs in honey

Asenfras mewn mel

The pig is such an accommodating animal. No wonder most rural Welsh households had one. Fed on scraps, the pig would be easily raised and fattened, then after the slaughter every bit of pork could be eaten, whether fresh, cured, smoked or pickled. What better way to use up those meaty ribs of pork than to cover them with a tangy sauce and roast, grill or barbecue them until sweet and tender?

4 tbsp clear honey
1 tbsp soy sauce
3 tbsp tomato ketchup
few drops Tabasco sauce
1 clove garlic, crushed with
  salt
salt to taste
1 tsp paprika
1 tsp mustard powder
juice and rind of 1 orange

4 tbsp wine vinegar
300 ml (½ pint) water, or
  water and white wine
  mixed
900 g (2 lb) Chinese-style
  (skinny) pork ribs

To garnish
12 Chinese spring onions (see
  below)

1. Mix the honey, soy sauce, tomato ketchup and Tabasco sauce in a bowl. Add garlic and season to taste with salt, paprika and mustard. Add grated orange rind, juice, wine vinegar and water.
2. Separate the ribs and soak in the sauce for at least 20 minutes in the fridge, turning from time to time.
3. Transfer the ribs and sauce to a large, oiled baking tray and bake in a hot oven (gas 7, 425°F, 220°C) for about 40 minutes, turning from time to time so that no rib burns, but all brown evenly.
4. Either serve the glistening ribs straight from the oven on a

large serving dish with the sauce poured over them, or finish
the cooking off on a barbecue to add the final crisp coating
and hand the sauce separately. Garnish with Chinese spring
onions and serve without cutlery . . . this is definitely a
fingers-only meal! In fact it might be a good idea to provide
finger bowls.

- For the Chinese spring onions – peel, top and tail them as
usual then cut into each end to a depth of 5 cm (2 in), like
the end of a party cracker. Soak in iced water for about 10
minutes so that the ends fan out into attractive curls.

M   Not suitable for microwave cookery

F   Not suitable for freezing

AP Prepare the recipe up to the end of stage 2

Welsh lamb chops with sweet herbs
Golwythion cig oen cymreig â safri fach

Savory fach, or winter savory as you may know it, marries well with the flavour of Welsh lamb. Growing in profusion on the hillsides of Wales it is a natural part of the lambs' diet, so flavouring their flesh with sweetness. In this recipe some savory is added to the chops before grilling to enhance the flavour.

4 tbsp olive oil
juice of ½ lemon
a good bunch of savory fach
   (winter savory) – or
   substitute thyme if
   unavailable

salt and freshly ground black
   pepper
8 good-sized lamb chops

To garnish
fresh savory or thyme

1. Mix the olive oil, lemon juice, finely chopped savory and seasoning. Pour over the chops and leave for at least 20 minutes in the fridge to marinate, longer if possible.
2. Cook the chops under a very hot grill so that they brown well on the outside but the middle is still pink. Turn once during grilling.
3. Serve immediately, garnished with sprigs of fresh herbs and accompanied by a leek and potato pie (see p. 222).

M   Not advisable for chops unless you can watch them very carefully and not overcook

F   Not suitable for freezing

AP Marinate the chops

Roast leg of lamb with ginger, honey, cider and rosemary

Coes cig oen gyda sinsir, mel, seidr a rhosmari

Sunday morning and the house is full of good smells, promises of things to come. Roast lamb, smothered in sweet spices and herbs, smells even better than most, and the flavour lives up to expectations!

'Butter was added to it, brown sugar, ginger and maybe something else. In a short time I was as warm as toast and glowing with geniality.' *Welsh Country Upbringing* by David Parry-Jones.

2.5 cm (1 in) piece of fresh root ginger
1 small leg of lamb, Welsh if possible, weighing about 1.35 k (3 lb)
25 g (1 oz) butter, melted
2 tbsp honey
1 tbsp fresh rosemary, chopped
100 ml (4 fl oz) cider
salt and freshly ground black pepper

1. Peel the ginger and cut it into slivers. Using a sharp knife make small cuts in the leg of lamb and insert the ginger.
2. Mix the butter, honey and rosemary together and spread this over the lamb. Put in a roasting tin, pour the cider in, and cover loosely with tinfoil.
3. Roast in a moderately hot oven (gas 6, 400°F, 200°C) allowing 15–20 minutes to the pound. When half cooked, remove the foil, and continue cooking, basting frequently with juices from the roasting tin.
4. Remove the joint from the oven, lift out of the pan and keep warm. Strain the juices from the pan, removing any excess fat, and pour in a little cider to 'deglaze' the pan. Boil this up well, return the non-fatty juices and thicken with a little arrowroot or kneaded butter (see p. 20).

M   Suitable for microwave cookery

F   Freeze well covered

AP Prepare up to the end of stage 2

Beef and ham loaf

Torth cig eidion a ham

Off to the Welsh hills with you, pack a picnic and take your stout walking shoes. This tasty meat loaf is ideal picnic fare. Served in thick slices with a spoonful of pickles it will sustain the most weary and footsore of hill walkers. Alternatively, serve it warm with a spicy tomato sauce or gravy for an economical family meal.

50 g (2 oz) stale bread
450 g (1 lb) lean beef, minced
225 g (8 oz) lean, rindless
  bacon, minced
1 medium onion, minced
1 clove garlic, crushed with
  1 tsp salt

2 tbsp parsley, chopped
50 g (2 oz) Caerphilly cheese
  grated
1 egg
freshly ground black pepper

1. Soak the stale bread in cold water for 5 minutes. Squeeze dry and mash well with a fork.
2. Mix all the ingredients together, working until smooth, and turn into a greased 450 g (1 lb) loaf tin. Cover with foil.
3. Place in a large roasting tin containing water to a depth of 2.5 cm (1 in). Bake in a moderate oven (gas 4, 350°F, 180°C) for about 1½ hours or until the loaf feels firm and has shrunk from the sides of the tin. Serve hot or cold with a sauce or pickles.

M   Suitable for microwave cookery (do not use foil)

F   Freezes well, covered; allow maximum thawing time to reconstitute texture fully

AP Make a day in advance and chill overnight. Reheat either in the microwave or well wrapped in foil in a moderate oven

Katt pie
Pastai Katt

No, this is not a pie of minced domestic pet, but a medieval-style mixture of mutton and currants. The origin of the name is a little vague, but Bobby Freeman, writing in *First Catch your Peacock*, suggests that it originates from Christopher Cat's Shire Lane pie-houses. The combination of meat and dried fruit is not uncommon, for before the fridge became a permanent fixture in our kitchens, meats were often cooked when pretty high in flavour, and sugar and dried fruit help to cover any 'off' tastes. Katt pies were traditionally sold at fairs throughout South Wales, and Templeton Fair, held annually in Pembrokeshire on 12 November, is particularly remembered for its wealth of Katt pies.

For the pastry
225 g (8 oz) flour
pinch of salt
50 g (2 oz) butter or hard
  margarine
50 g (2 oz) lard
cold water to bind

For the filling
50 g (2 oz) currants
50 g (2 oz) soft brown sugar
225 g (8 oz) lean minced lamb
salt and freshly ground black
  pepper

1. Make up the shortcrust pastry: sift the flour and salt into a large bowl. Using your fingertips, rub the butter and lard, cut into cubes, into the flour until the mixture resembles fine breadcrumbs – make sure you lift your hands well above the bowl so that air is incorporated into the mixture and the warmth of your hands doesn't cause the fats to melt in the bottom of the bowl. Add just enough cold water to bind, and stir with a palette knife until the dough is well amalgamated. Chill for 30 minutes then turn it on to a table top lightly dusted

with flour and roll out. Rotate the circle of dough as you roll it out, so that it never becomes stuck to the table and you end up with an even disc of manageable pastry.

2. Use two thirds of the pastry to line a plate or pie dish about 20–25 cm (8–10 in) diameter. Arrange the filling in the dish in layers of currants, sugar, minced lamb and seasoning.

3. Cover the pie with the remaining pastry cut into a lid, dampening the edges to seal. Press the lid down well on to the dampened pastry and using your thumb crimp the edge.

4. Brush with a little cold milk to glaze, and bake for about 40 minutes in a moderately hot oven (gas 5, 375°F, 190°C) until golden brown.

• An alternative way to cook and serve Katt pie is to make up 12 individual pies in a Yorkshire pudding tin.

M   Suitable for microwave cookery

F   Freezes well

AP Prepare pastry and filling. Combine the two when ready to cook

Loin of pork Llandeilo
Llwyn o borc Llandeilo

Loin of pork has a fine flavour of its own, but mixed with fresh sage, ground allspice and a little garlic, it's magnificent. Sage is one of the survivors in my garden. When lack of care and attention kill off parsley, basil, dill and marjoram, my sage never wavers but just keeps on growing. David Hoffman writes in *Welsh Herbal Medicine* (1978): 'Sage is useful when boiled to strengthen the nerves . . . It is a good thing for those in health to drink half a draught in the morning in order to preserve health and prolong life.'

1.35 k (3 lb) loin of pork, boned and de-rinded (see p. 18 and follow instructions for lamb; or ask your butcher to do it)
salt and freshly ground black pepper
2 fresh sage leaves, chopped, plus extra for the gravy

½ tsp ground allspice
1 clove of garlic
150 ml (¼ pint) dry white wine
1 tbsp flour
300 ml (½ pint) vegetable stock

1. Put the pork in a large dish and rub with salt, pepper, sage and allspice. Leave in a cool place for several hours or overnight.
2. Cut the garlic into slivers and insert at intervals along the joint. Roll, and tie up with string or strong thread.
3. Put in a roasting tin and pour on the wine. Cover with foil and roast in a warm oven (gas 3, 325°F, 170°C) for 2½ hours. If all the liquid evaporates during cooking, add a little more wine.
4. When the loin is cooked remove from the pan, drain off any

excess fat and stir the flour into the pan juices. Let this boil up well, stirring all the time, then pour in the vegetable stock to make a gravy. Adjust the seasoning, adding a little more wine if necessary and perhaps some more freshly chopped sage.

- Serve with buttered boiled potatoes and perhaps a spinach, herb and mushroom mould (see p. 223).

M   Suitable for microwave cookery

F   Freeze spiced joint of fresh pork prior to cooking or freeze cooked loin whole or in slices. Freeze gravy separately

AP   Prepare up to the end of stage 2

Rack of lamb with lavender

Cig oen gyda lafant

This must be my favourite way to cook and serve lamb. Simple, inexpensive and delicious. The sweet flavour and succulence of the meat is maximized by roasting the rack quickly in a very hot oven. Yves Monin first introduced me to cooking lavender with lamb when I ate at his delightful little restaurant, The Bakestone, in Caernarfon. Every meal eaten there is a delicious experience but his lamb with lavender was particularly memorable.

Cream cheese flavoured with garlic and herbs has been available for many years in Britain, but Plas Farm on Anglesey have produced an extremely good and creamy one. Use it if you can, or substitute your own favourite.

Most supermarkets now sell rack of lamb but if in doubt ask the butcher for a best end of neck which has not been cut into chops.

1 tsp fresh lavender (or
   substitute rosemary)
75 g (3 oz) garlic-flavoured
   cream cheese
50 g (2 oz) brown
   breadcrumbs

675–900 g (1½–2 lb) best end
   of neck of lamb, skinned
   and chined (see p. 19), or
   ask your butcher to do it)

1. Chop the lavender finely or grind it to a powder, and mix with the cream cheese and breadcrumbs. Press this mixture together with a palette knife and spread over the fat side of the lamb.
2. Put the rack of lamb in a roasting tin and cook in a hot oven (gas 7, 425°F, 220°C) for 30 minutes, or a little longer if you don't like your lamb pink.

3. Serve the lamb cut down between the rib bones either as single cutlets or doubles. The meat will be deliciously juicy and the garlic topping will give a crisp outside to each cutlet.

● No sauce is necessary, simply serve a moist vegetable dish such as leek and carrot medley (see p. 201) as an accompaniment.

M   Not suitable for microwave cookery

F   Not suitable for freezing

AP   Make up the garlic mixture and spread it over the lamb

DISHES WITHOUT MEAT

Carrot and leek medley
Punchnep
Cheese and apple potato cake
Parsnip pie
Parsnip and lentil pots
Oatmeal dumplings
Pasta with wild mushrooms
Cheesy leek tarts
Cheese pudding
Celtic pie
Caerphilly and mushroom pancake
Broad beans in sour cream
Onion cake
Leek and potato pie
Spinach, herb and mushroom mould
Stuffed vine leaves
Welsh rarebit
Croffta leeks
Pumpkin in cheese sauce
Spinach pancakes
Glamorgan sausages
Green salad with honey dressing

The growing number of vegetarians would appreciate life in Wales today. There is a large increase in the production of organic vegetables throughout the principality and these are usually sold extremely fresh in local markets. This chapter has a surprisingly large number of composite vegetable dishes and is particularly aimed at vegetarians. As visitors to Wales they can be assured of a fine welcome and dishes to suit their tastes.

Many people today do not feel the need for meat at every meal. For most of us, a Sunday roast, perhaps two or three quick meat dishes during the week and some fish dishes make up the average weekly diet. Cheese, eggs and vegetables can be combined to provide tasty lunches or light suppers without any need for meat at all. Perhaps, though, the biggest change in our eating habits has been due to the influx of exotic foods into Britain from all corners of the world, and in our excitement to try the huge range of new tastes, meat is playing a less important role in our diet. We know that cereals and vegetables are important for our general well-being, and for those who still find eating vegetables a duty rather than a pleasure I hope that the following recipes will provide a little encouragement.

Glamorgan sausages, for example, combine the traditional appearance of a sausage with an unusual and tasty middle of leeks and cheese. Serve them with a tomato sauce and you have an adaptable dish, suitable for a snack, light lunch or supper, or even the first course of a formal dinner.

Combining root vegetables to make punchnep has always been a tradition with the Welsh. It is so easy to boil potatoes with turnips, swede or parsnips and mash them together. Don't forget to add a knob of butter or spoonful of cream at the end to give the punchnep that wonderful rich flavour.

Punchnep offers another asset to the busy cook, who can prepare two vegetables in one dish and so save time and energy. By the same token why not try carrot and leek medley for a colourful and convenient dish?

Lastly, don't overlook the adaptability of the salad. Fresh, crunchy salad vegetables are available all the year round, so find a dressing that suits you, perhaps the honey one in this chapter, and change the salad ingredients throughout the year.

Carrot and leek medley

Miri moron a chennin

How many of us have the time or patience to prepare three or four fresh vegetables as accompaniments to meat? Yet potatoes and one other vegetable make for uninteresting dining if served too regularly. Here is an idea that is simple, colourful and combines the flavours and textures of two vegetables. Do try it; it looks spectacular and tastes delicious.

450 g (1 lb) leeks, finely chopped – choose slim young ones if possible
225 g (½ lb) carrots, grated

salt and freshly ground black pepper
25 (1 oz) butter
4 tbsp water

1. Combine the vegetables in an ovenproof dish and season well. Cut the butter into slivers, distribute over the top and add the water.
2. Bake, covered, for 30 minutes in a moderate oven (gas 4, 350°F, 180°C) until the leeks and carrots are cooked but still just crunchy.
3. Fluff up the vegetables with a fork to lighten the texture and serve immediately before they lose their bright colour.

M   Reduce water to 2 tbsp and cook for 10 minutes on high

F   Not suitable for freezing

AP Prepare up to the end of stage 1

Punchnep

A mash of root vegetables, now a fashionable dish to serve with formal meals, has always been a favourite in Wales. Potatoes and baby white turnips are the traditional mix for punchnep but there are many alternatives such as swedes, peas, parsnips or carrots which can all be mashed together or individually with potatoes. If you have any left over, punchnep makes a superb morning-after fry up with a rasher or two of bacon. Very traditional and very good.

450 g (1 lb) potatoes, peeled
450 g (1 lb) baby turnips, scrubbed, topped and tailed
50 g (2 oz) butter
salt and freshly ground black pepper

50 ml (2 fl oz) cream, buttermilk or yogurt (optional)

To garnish
chopped parsley

1. Cut the potatoes and turnips into chunks about 2.5 cm (1 in) diameter. Put in a large pan of cold, salted water, bring to the boil and simmer until tender.
2. Drain the cooked vegetables and whilst still warm mash together with the butter and plenty of seasoning.
3. Serve the punchnep as it is or for a real treat stir in some cream, buttermilk or yogurt. Garnish with the parsley.

M   Microwave as for potatoes

F   Freeze covered, reheat from frozen

AP Cook up to the end of stage 2. Reheat with a thin layer of cream or melted butter spread over the top to stop a crust forming, and mash the cream in just before serving

Cheese and apple potato cake

Teisennau afalau caws a thatws

This is the perfect dish to prepare with a roast of Welsh lamb or pork, or a casserole such as harvest hot pot (see p. 170). Alternatively you can eat it on its own, warm with sweet pickles, or cut the dough into scones with a pastry cutter and serve buttered.

450 g (1 lb) potatoes, peeled
100 g (4 oz) self-raising flour
25 g (1 oz) melted butter
pinch of mixed spice
1 egg
100 ml (¼ pint) milk, or
  slightly less

For the filling
2 good-sized cooking apples,
  peeled
1 large onion, peeled
50 g (2 oz) soft brown sugar
75 g (3 oz) well-flavoured
  farmhouse Cheddar
salt and freshly ground black
  pepper

1. Boil the potatoes in salted water. Mash, leave to cool, then mix with the flour, butter, spice, egg and enough milk to make a soft dough.
2. Roll the dough into a large rectangle approximately 20 cm × 30 cm (8 in × 12 in). Grate the apple and onion over half of the dough and sprinkle over the sugar, cheese and seasoning. Dampen the edges of the dough, fold over the uncovered end and seal.
3. Bake this large turnover on a greased baking tray in a moderate oven (gas 4, 350°F, 180°C) for 40 minutes until golden brown.
4. If preparing scones stir the apple filling into the dough, roll out and cut with a pastry cutter. Bake for 15 minutes in a moderately hot oven (gas 5, 375°F, 190°C).

M   Cook as for scones

F   Freezes well

AP   Prepare the potatoes, mash and cool. Finish the recipe when required

Parsnip pie
Pastai pannas

Before the advent of sugar in our everyday diet parsnips were used to sweeten many dishes. If carrots can find their way into cakes, and pumpkins into pies, then should we not make more of the succulent parsnip?

This pie is a wicked combination of sweet parsnips with tomatoes, cream and well-flavoured Welsh Teifi cheese. Produced on the farm at Llandyssul in Dyfed, this Gouda-type cheese is made from unpasteurized milk and has a good bite and texture.

4 tbsp sunflower or rapeseed oil

900 g (2 lb) parsnips, peeled and thinly sliced

50 g (2 oz) butter

salt and freshly ground black pepper

300 ml (½ pint) single cream

450 g (1 lb) tomatoes, skinned (see p. 21), deseeded and sliced

175 g (6 oz) Teifi cheese, grated (or substitute Gouda)

4 tbsp fresh wholemeal breadcrumbs

1. Heat the oil in a pan and lightly fry the parsnips for 4 minutes.
2. Grease a 1.2 l (2 pint) casserole dish with half the butter and place a layer of parsnips over the base. Sprinkle with salt and pepper and add a little cream before covering with a layer of tomatoes. Spread a little more cream and some cheese over the tomatoes and repeat these layers until all the ingredients are used up, finishing off with cream and cheese. Top with the breadcrumbs and dot with the remaining butter.
3. Cook for 30 minutes in the centre of a moderately hot oven (gas 6, 400°F, 200°C) until cooked through and crisp on top.

M   Cook in the microwave and crisp under the grill to finish

F   The appearance may suffer with freezing if the crispness is lost from the top

AP Prepare to end of stage 2

Parsnip and lentil pots

Potiau pannas a chorbys

The flavour of parsnips is improved with a touch of frost, so delay trying this recipe until late autumn if you can. The sweetness of their flesh, rather like pumpkin, adds a special flavour to this vegetable dish. Lentils have been in great demand in Wales over the past century with the increase of the immigrant population, and nowhere more so than the cosmopolitan docklands of Cardiff.

900 g (2 lb) parsnips, thinly sliced
75 g (3 oz) green lentils
75 g (3 oz) brown rice
25 g (1 oz) butter
1 small onion, chopped
1 tbsp flour
600 ml (1 pint) milk
nutmeg to taste
salt and freshly ground black pepper
1 tbsp melted butter

1. Blanch the parsnips by covering with cold water in a saucepan, bringing to the boil, and simmering for 2 minutes. Drain.
2. Combine the lentils and rice in a large saucepan. Cover with cold water, bring to the boil and simmer for 35 minutes until just cooked.
3. Meanwhile, make the sauce: melt the butter in a saucepan, sauté the onion for 2–3 minutes then add the flour and cook, stirring, for 1–2 minutes. Add the milk slowly, stirring all the time. Bring to the boil and simmer until thickened. Add nutmeg and seasoning to taste.
4. Butter a 1.7 l (3 pint) ovenproof dish or some individual ramekin dishes and spoon alternate layers of parsnips, lentil and rice mixture and sauce into each dish. Finish with a layer of sauce and some parsnip slices.

5. Brush lightly with melted butter and bake in a moderate
   oven (gas 4, 350°F, 180°C) until golden brown – 40 minutes
   for a large dish or 20 minutes for the ramekins.

M Suitable for microwave cookery; brown under a grill to
   finish

F The texture may become very stodgy when frozen

AP Prepare up to the end of stage 4

Oatmeal dumplings
Twmplenni blawd ceirch

An old traditional dish of rural Wales, these dumplings, or trollies, were eaten with cawl or stews. Some fat would be skimmed from the top of the stew and mixed with the oatmeal to form a dough. This was shaped into dumplings and added to the pot to cook through during the last half hour or so of cooking. Delicious, these dumplings, in fact I believe they were sometimes kept for pudding to eat with custard!

100 g (4 oz) suet (animal or vegetarian)
100 g (4 oz) self-raising flour
100 g (4 oz) currants

450 g (1 lb) fine oatmeal
pinch of salt
350 ml (12 fl oz) milk, or buttermilk if available

1. Mix together the suet, flour, currants, oatmeal and salt and add enough milk to make a firm dough.
2. On a lightly floured board roll into small balls of 5 cm (2 in) diameter and poach the dumplings for 20 minutes in a large saucepan of gently simmering water, or steam them on top of a casserole for the last 30 minutes of cooking time. Serve warm with savoury or sweet dishes.

M   Dumplings are a real success in the microwave. Cook for about 5 minutes

F   Not suitable for freezing

AP –

Pasta with wild mushrooms
Pasta gyda madarch gwyllt

Chanterelles are commonplace in the woods deep in the very heart of Wales. At the Lake Hotel in Llangammarch Wells they were first discovered by a German visitor five years ago, and such was his excitement that he returned to the hotel for a bucket in which to collect his supper. If you have no such opportunity, oyster mushrooms, cèpes, flat field mushrooms and even the dried boletus mushrooms available from Italian delicatessens will achieve an almost equally fine flavour.

225 g (8 oz) wholewheat pasta spirals
1 tbsp olive oil
1 small onion, finely chopped
1 clove garlic, crushed with salt
225 g (8 oz) wild mushrooms, sliced – chanterelles, cèpes, morels, oyster, field or dried boletus mushrooms (reconstituted in water)
2 medium tomatoes, skinned, seeded and sliced (see p. 21)

100 ml (4 fl oz) dry white wine
150 ml (5 fl oz) single cream
1 tbsp fresh lovage or parsley, chopped
salt and freshly ground black pepper

To garnish
chopped parsley

1. Cook the pasta with a drop of oil in a large pan of boiling salted water.
2. Meanwhile heat the tbsp oil in a large, heavy-based casserole and gently fry the onion and garlic over a moderate heat for 5 minutes until soft and translucent. Add the sliced mushrooms and chopped tomatoes and cook for another 2 minutes, stirring constantly.

3. Stir in the wine, boil up for 1 minute, then reduce the heat and add the cream, herbs and seasoning.
4. When the pasta is cooked, drain and mix immediately into the mushroom sauce. Serve direct from the casserole, garnished with the chopped parsley and accompanied by chunks of fresh bread.

M Cook the sauce in the microwave while the pasta cooks conventionally

F Not suitable for freezing

AP –

Cheesy leek tarts

Teisennau caws a chennin

These little cheesy leek tarts are ideal picnic fare, just the thing to pack in a hamper or rucksack. Their robust flavour will survive any ordeal, and should you set out to climb the 3,560 feet of Mount Snowdon they'll taste all the better for reaching the summit. Alas, their flavour will, I fear, be a little impaired if you go by train . . . you lazy thing!

Makes 12–15

For the pastry
3 tbsp oil
pinch of salt
6 tbsp hot water
175 g (6 oz) wholemeal flour

– or substitute shortcrust or
 puff pastry

To garnish
sprigs of watercress
tomato slices

For the filling
2 medium leeks, finely
 chopped
50 g (2 oz) butter
1 tbsp fresh basil, chopped
1 tbsp flour
150 g (5 oz) cream cheese
150 ml (5 fl oz) sour cream
1 tsp made mustard
salt and freshly ground black
 pepper
50 g (2 oz) mature farmhouse
 cheese, grated
1 tbsp sesame seeds

1. Make up the pastry by mixing the oil, salt and water together then gradually adding the flour until a pliable dough is formed. Cool then roll out and cut into circles with a 7.5 cm (3 in) pastry cutter. Use to line bun tins and bake blind in a moderately hot oven (gas 5, 375°F, 190°C) for 15 minutes or until lightly coloured.
2. For the filling, fry the leeks in the butter with the basil until

soft. Stir in the flour then, off the heat, add the cream cheese, sour cream, mustard and seasoning. It should be a very thick mixture. Cool for 30 minutes before spooning into the pastry cases.

3. Sprinkle grated cheese and sesame seeds over the top of each tart and cook in a hot oven (gas 7, 425°F, 220°C) for about 10 minutes until the cheese is golden brown.

4. Serve immediately with a garnish of watercress and tomato, or cool to pack in a rucksack.

M   Not suitable for microwave cookery

F   Suitable for freezing

AP Cook in advance, reheat in a warm (not hot) oven to serve

Cheese pudding

Pwdin caws

A guaranteed success with the Welsh, this economical, tasty and filling cheese pudding contains everything they enjoy. Dairy products – butter, milk and cheese – mixed together with egg, spices and bread. Try using a Sage Derby, Cheddar with chives or Gruyère to alter the flavour.

A similar dish can be found in the Alps where a drop or two of wine soaked into the bread makes a subtle difference.

6 thick slices wholemeal bread, crusts removed	salt and cayenne pepper good pinch grated nutmeg
50 g (2 oz) butter	600 ml (1 pint) milk
350 g (12 oz) mature farmhouse Cheddar, grated	1 egg ½ tsp English mustard

1. Toast the bread on one side only. Butter the untoasted side.
2. Butter a large, shallow, ovenproof dish and arrange half the bread, toasted side down, on the bottom. Sprinkle over half the cheese, season well with salt, cayenne pepper and nutmeg, then add the rest of the bread, toasted side down, and sprinkle the remaining cheese on top.
3. Mix the milk with the egg and mustard, pour over the bread and cheese and grate some nutmeg on top. Leave the pudding for 30 minutes to allow the milk to soak into the bread.
4. Scrape a few slivers of butter over the top and bake in a medium oven (gas 4, 350°F, 180°C) for 30 minutes. Serve immediately.
• A salad of tomatoes and chives would make a good accompaniment to this dish.

M   Not suitable; a microwave won't give the same crusty finish

F   Not suitable for freezing

AP Prepare up to the end of stage 3

Celtic pie
Pastai geltaidd

Eluned Lloyd serves this dish regularly in her guesthouse in Newport where she and her family are keen to demonstrate the best in authentic Welsh recipes, using local organically produced ingredients wherever possible.

For the oaten crusty base
100 g (4 oz) margarine
2 tbsp water
100 g (4 oz) oats
75 g (3 oz) wholemeal flour
pinch of salt

For the filling
2 tomatoes, sliced
1 tsp fresh tarragon (or other herbs)
1 onion, sliced into rings
olive oil for frying
100–175 g (4–6 oz) farmhouse cheese, sliced

219 g (7½ oz) tin of laverbread, (or substitute cooked and chopped spinach)
juice and zest of 1 orange
150 ml (5 fl oz) natural yogurt
2 eggs
4 tbsp tinned sweetcorn
salt and freshly ground black pepper

To garnish
1 orange, peeled and segmented

1. First make the base: melt the margarine, add the water, then the oats, flour and salt. Stir briskly and use to line a 21 cm (8½ in) flan dish by pressing the mixture with the back of a spoon or your fingers.
2. Arrange the sliced tomatoes on the base of the flan and sprinkle with a favourite herb. Fry the onion rings in a little olive oil and place on top of the tomatoes. Cover with slices of cheese.

3. In a bowl, mix together the laverbread, orange juice and zest, yogurt, eggs and sweetcorn. Pour this mixture over the cheese. Season.

4. Bake in a moderately hot oven (gas 6, 400°F, 200°C) for 40–45 minutes until the mixture is set. Garnish with chunks of orange and serve hot or cold.

M   Will adjust to microwave cookery, but crisp under the grill before serving

F   Not suitable for freezing

AP Prepare up to the end of stage 2

Caerphilly and mushroom pancake
Crempog Caerffili

Here is another favourite Welsh way to serve the ever popular
pancake. They are layered into a stack which is then cut in slices
like a cake. This is an economical meal, and the fillings can be
altered to suit your taste. Caerphilly is a particularly good
cheese to use since it cooks well, but any mild-flavoured cheese
would do. The use of beer in the batter not only gives a pleasant
taste but lightens the consistency.

For the batter
150 ml (¼ pint) milk
150 ml (¼ pint) light ale or
  lager
2 eggs
1 tbsp melted butter
100 g (4 oz) wholemeal flour

For the fillings
225 g (8 oz) Caerphilly
  cheese, grated

150 ml (¼ pint) double cream
salt and cayenne or chilli
  pepper
1 large or 2 medium leeks,
  finely chopped
25 g (1 oz) butter
175 g (6 oz) flat field
  mushrooms, sliced

1. Put the ingredients for the batter in a liquidizer in the order
   listed and whizz until smooth. Leave to stand for 30 minutes.
2. For the first filling, mix 175 g (6 oz) of the cheese with the
   cream and season well with the cayenne pepper and a little
   salt.
3. For the second filling, fry the leeks in the butter for 4 minutes
   then add the mushrooms and cook for another 3 minutes.
   Season well.
4. Heat a 20 cm (8 in) frying pan and make about twelve thin
   pancakes (see p. 21). Don't worry if the first pancake tears;

remember that it can sit unnoticed at the bottom of the dish, and by the time you get to the top of the pile your pancakes will no doubt be perfect.

5. Butter a heatproof dish and lay a pancake flat on the bottom. Then, alternating the fillings of cheese and cream or mushroom and leek, pile up the pancakes flat on top of each other.

6. The final result should look like a pancake dome. Sprinkle the remaining cheese over, put a knob of butter on top and bake in a hot oven (gas 7, 425°F, 220°C) for 15 minutes, or grill gently for 10 minutes.

M   The leek and mushroom filling could be prepared in the microwave

F   Not advisable for a special meal but OK for freezing a leftover portion

AP Prepare up to the end of stage 5

Broad beans in sour cream
Ffa mewn hufen sur

When broad beans are in season it is wise to use them in every possible way, for the frozen ones are nothing like as good. This is a clever way to serve broad beans, the sour cream gives the dish a certain tang and the crisp topping appeals to everyone. Serve with Rack of Lamb with Lavender (see p. 195) and the moisture of this dish will complement the crisp succulence of the lamb.

450 g (1 lb) broad beans (shelled weight)
150 ml (5 fl oz) sour cream
salt and freshly ground black pepper
grated nutmeg
½ tsp caraway or dill seeds
50 g (2 oz) butter
50 g (2 oz) fresh white breadcrumbs

1. Blanch the beans by cooking them in boiling water for 2 minutes then refreshing them immediately under the cold tap.
2. Mix the sour cream with the salt, pepper, nutmeg and caraway seeds. Add the beans and transfer to a heatproof dish.
3. Melt the butter, stir in the breadcrumbs and arrange over the beans. Bake in a moderate oven (gas 4, 350°F, 180°C) for 15–20 minutes or until the topping is crisp and brown.

M   Will adapt to microwave cookery, but brown under the grill to finish

F   Not advisable because of the sour cream sauce

AP Prepare in advance; cook when required

Onion cake

Teisen nionod

Like many potato and onion dishes this consists of alternate layers of the two vegetables. The difference is that this really is a cake, baked in a cake tin and turned out to look rather special.

1 bay leaf
900 g (2 lb) potatoes, peeled
   and finely sliced into cold
   water to prevent
   discoloration

225 g (8 oz) onions, peeled
   and finely sliced
75 g (3 oz) butter, melted
salt and freshly ground black
   pepper

1. Butter an 18 cm (7 in) deep cake tin and put the bay leaf in the bottom.
2. Place a layer of potatoes over the base. Add a layer of onions, brush with melted butter and season well with salt and pepper. Continue these layers, finishing with a layer of potatoes.
3. *Press the cake down well into the tin*, brush the top with butter and cover with foil. Bake in a hot oven (gas 7, 425°F, 220°C) for about one hour or until the potatoes are soft. Remove the foil for the last 10 minutes to brown the surface. Turn the cake out to serve.

- Grated cheese could be added to the onion cake to give it a more substantial flavour.

M Much of the colour will be lost in microwave cookery, so for preference cook it in a conventional oven

F The texture may not be as good after freezing

AP Make in advance and cook for 45 minutes. Reheat when required, allowing 30 minutes to complete the cooking

Leek and potato pie
Pastai cennin a thatws

The perfect vegetable dish. It is no trouble to prepare, uses inexpensive ingredients, never spoils with overcooking, and has a really good flavour too. Slices of pretty green leeks make this a most attractive vegetable dish. Serve it with everything from Lamb and Mint Sausages to Salt Duck, or serve it on its own and enjoy its individual flavour.

675 g (1½ lb) potatoes	salt and freshly ground black
2 slim leeks, sliced	pepper
50 g (2 oz) butter	300 ml (½ pint) vegetable
	stock

1. Peel and slice the potatoes thinly. Put them straight into cold water to stop the colour spoiling and allow some of the starch to disperse.
2. Arrange the leeks and potatoes in layers in a pie dish greased with some of the butter, adding salt and pepper to each layer and finishing with a decorative layer of potatoes on top.
3. Dot the remaining butter over and pour in the stock. Bake in a moderate oven (gas 4, 350°F, 180°C) for one hour or until the potatoes are tender and the top browned.

M   Cook in the microwave, brown under the grill to finish

F   Not suitable for freezing

AP Prepare the pie and cook for 30 minutes. Finish the cooking just before serving

Spinach, herb and mushroom mould

Cylch madarch, perlysiau a phigoglys

Fashionable as it now is to cultivate our own herb gardens, herbs played a far greater part in the lives of the Welsh in the past. Apothecaries employed herb gatherers to wander the countryside collecting herbs to be made into healing potions. To purify the air herbs were strewn over the floor, mixed in pot pourris, distilled into oils and scents. In Elizabethan times the grander houses would have a large part of their walled vegetable gardens devoted to herbs and women were employed solely to collect, prepare, dry and distil the herbs in a still room.

900 g (2 lb) fresh spinach
2 eggs
1 tbsp cream, single or double
salt and freshly ground black
    pepper

2 tbsp fresh herbs – chervil,
    lovage or marjoram
1 tsp nutmeg, freshly grated
225 g (8 oz) mushrooms,
    sliced
50 g (2 oz) butter

1. Wash the spinach very well and cook in a minimum of water for about 5 minutes, drain thoroughly, and chop. (If possible cook in a non-metallic pan or casserole, it doesn't affect the acid so much.)
2. Beat the eggs into the spinach, then add the cream, seasoning, herbs and nutmeg.
3. Fry the mushrooms gently in the butter for 3 minutes. Butter a 1.2 l (2 pint) mould, heatproof bowl or pyrex dish and scatter half of the mushrooms on the bottom. Cover with half the spinach, followed by a final layer of mushrooms before covering with the rest of the spinach.
4. Cover the dish with foil or a lid and stand it in a roasting tin

holding 2.5 cm (1 in) of water (a *bain-marie*). Bake in a moderate oven (gas 4, 350°F, 180°C) for 30 minutes until firm to the touch. Alternatively, use 4 small moulds and bake for only 15 minutes.

5. Turn out on to a serving dish and serve on its own or as a vegetable dish with meat or fish.

M   Suitable for microwave cookery

F   Not suitable; the eggs will make the texture leathery

AP   Prepare up to the end of stage 3

Stuffed vine leaves
Dail gwinwydd wedi'u stwffio

With four vineyards producing wine on a commercial basis in Wales we can boast a certain self-sufficiency, away from the wine lakes of the EEC. Alas our climate is erratic and some years the vines yield better crops than others, but even if the grapes are few the vine leaves always flourish. This delicious recipe comes from Dr Idris Thomas at his Wern Deg Vineyard in Dyfed.

8 fresh vine leaves, or 1 packet blanched vine leaves
100 g (4 oz) cooked rice
25 g (1 oz) sultanas
50 g (2 oz) walnuts, chopped
pinch of nutmeg
1 egg, beaten
25 g (1 oz) cooked lentils (optional)

1 clove garlic, crushed with salt
300 ml (½ pt) stock or water
50 ml (2 fl oz) single cream
2 egg yolks
1 tsp cornflour
juice of ½ lemon
salt and freshly ground black pepper

For the sauce
2 tbsp vegetable oil
1 small onion, chopped

To garnish
lemon wedges

1. For fresh vine leaves, blanch for 4 minutes in boiling water then rinse under the cold tap and drain well.
2. Mix all the remaining ingredients for the filling and divide between the prepared vine leaves. Parcel neatly and pack closely into a casserole with a lid.
3. For the sauce: heat the oil in a saucepan and fry the onion and garlic gently for 3 minutes. Add the stock and simmer for another 3 minutes.

4. Mix cream, egg yolks and cornflour together in a bowl and add gradually to the stock. Bring to the boil, stirring until the sauce thickens then add the lemon juice. Season to taste.

5. Pour the sauce over the vine leaves and bake in a moderate oven (gas 4, 350°F, 180°C) for about 20 minutes until hot right through. Serve garnished with seedless green grapes and lemon wedges.

M   Suitable for microwave cookery

F   Not suitable for freezing

AP   Prepare up to the end of stage 2. Make up the sauce at time of cooking

Welsh rarebit

Caws pob

How the Welsh have always loved 'roasted cheese', even since medieval times. Alas, good, hard, strong-flavoured, Cheddar-type cheese has not always been produced in Wales, since the acidity of the soil leads towards a softer texture and flavour. During times of poverty only skimmed milk was available for cheesemaking, but during the last century the combination of ewe's milk and cow's milk made a much better cheese, and so the perfect Welsh rarebit could be prepared to satisfy the Welsh taste.

This is the most palatable of dishes. Eat Welsh rarebit for breakfast, elevenses, lunch, tea, supper, or as a savoury course at the end of dinner!

225 g (8 oz) strong-flavoured Cheddar
25 g (1 oz) butter, melted
1 tbsp Worcestershire sauce
1 tbsp English mustard
1 tbsp flour
4 tbsp beer
4 slices wholemeal toast
cayenne pepper

1. Grate the cheese and mix with the remaining ingredients to a firm paste.
2. Spread over the 4 slices of toast and grill gently until the topping is cooked through and well-browned.

M   Not necessary

F   Possible if you need to prepare a large amount in advance

AP Prepare in advance and cook when required

Croffta Leeks
Cennin Groffta

Here is a medieval recipe for leeks prepared in an eastern Mediterranean manner, hinting at its Roman origin. They are known as Slit Sops but I have amended the title to encompass the flavour of wine made in Wales. Croffta is produced just outside Cardiff at Groes Faen, using a combination of Seyve-Villard and Müller-Thurgau grapes to produce a wine that is crisp and dry. The mixture of Croffta wine and olive oil in which the leeks are cooked is delicious and I suggest that you serve lots of crisp French or coarse brown bread with this dish so that none of the delicious juices are wasted.

450 g (1 lb) slim young leeks
5 tbsp olive oil
225 ml (8 fl oz) dry white wine

salt and freshly ground black pepper

1. Peel the outer layer off the leeks and cut off the roots. Wash them very thoroughly under the cold tap and drain well.
2. Combine the oil, wine and seasoning in a saucepan or ovenproof dish large enough to fit in the whole leeks. Simmer on the stove or poach in a moderate oven (gas 4, 350°F, 180°C) for about 25 minutes or until the leeks are tender, then leave to cool in the cooking liquid.
• Serve warm or cold, with a meat dish such as Dark Age Chicken (p. 139) or as a first course with chunks of fresh granary bread.

M   Suitable for microwave cookery

F   Not suitable for freezing

AP   Cook the entire dish, reheat gently when required, or serve
     cold

Pumpkin in cheese sauce

Pwmpen mewn saws caws

If you think that the Americans discovered the pumpkin then let me tell you that it became famous on the Gower peninsula well before it was exported across the Atlantic, according to Bobby Freeman who has researched deeply into cookery from the Gower. The sweet flesh of the pumpkin blends well with the acid sharpness of a fine Caerphilly cheese.

900 g (2 lb) pumpkin, skinned, deseeded and sliced
25 g (1 oz) butter or margarine
25 g (1 oz) flour

300 ml (½ pint) milk
100 g (4 oz) Caerphilly, grated
salt and freshly ground black pepper
½ tsp cayenne
1 tbsp sesame seeds

1. Drop the pumpkin slices into a large pan of boiling water and simmer for five minutes. Drain.
2. For the cheese sauce, melt the butter in a saucepan, stir in the flour, then gradually add the milk and bring to the boil. When the sauce has thickened, add the cheese and seasoning.
3. Arrange the pumpkin slices in a shallow ovenproof dish and pour the cheese sauce over.
4. Scatter the sesame seeds on top and bake in a hot oven (gas 7, 425°F, 220°C) for 20 minutes.
• Serve on its own or to accompany a meat dish.

M   Will adapt to microwave cooking but brown under a grill to finish

F   Not recommended. The pumpkin will become very watery when frozen

AP Prepare up to the end of stage 3

Spinach pancakes
Crempogau pigoglys

Spinach is used by the Italians for colouring pasta as well as to add flavour. On the same principle, cooked spinach is added to pancake batter in this recipe. A sauce can be served with these pancakes, but I think that they look terrific on their own, with a crisp outer shell covering a low-fat filling.

For the batter
100 g (4 oz) flour
1 egg
1 yolk
300 ml (½ pint) liquid (almost all milk but add a dash of water)
1 tbsp sunflower or rapeseed oil
2 tbsp cooked spinach, chopped
salt and freshly ground black pepper

For the filling
225 g (8 oz) low-fat curd cheese
225 g (8 oz) cooked spinach, chopped
25 g (1 oz) pine nuts or sunflower seeds

25 g (1 oz) fresh Parmesan cheese, grated
salt, freshly ground black pepper, freshly grated nutmeg

To garnish
25 g (1 oz) toasted pine nuts or sunflower seeds – to toast, simply heat gently in a frying pan, in the oven or under a medium grill until brown – this always takes longer than you anticipate. Nuts brown well in the microwave too; place them directly on the turntable dish and stir from time to time.

1. Put all the ingredients for the batter in a liquidizer and whizz until smooth.

2. For the filling, mix all the ingredients, blend together well.
3. In a lightly greased 20 cm (8 in) frying pan fry thin pancakes (see p. 21) and stack to keep them moist.
4. Spoon the filling into the pancakes, fold and arrange in a heatproof dish.
5. Bake in a hot oven (gas 7, 425°F, 220°C) for 15 minutes or put under a medium grill for 15 minutes.
6. Serve the pancakes piping hot with a crunchy garnish of toasted nuts or seeds scattered over the top.

M   Once prepared, these pancakes could be reheated in the microwave

F   Not advisable since the curd cheese will separate

AP Prepare up to the end of stage 4

Glamorgan sausages
Selsig morgannwg

This is a recipe for the original vegetarian sausage. Containing cheese, breadcrumbs, leeks and herbs, these tasty sausages were mentioned by George Borrow in his book, *Wild Wales*, written in 1862. Alas, Glamorgan cheese, from which they got their name, is no longer made, but Caerphilly is thought to be a direct descendant and gives these sausages a fine texture and flavour.

150 g (5 oz) fresh
   breadcrumbs, plus 75–100 g
   (3–4 oz) for coating
1 small leek, very finely
   chopped
75 g (3 oz) Caerphilly cheese,
   grated
1 tbsp fresh parsley, chopped
salt and freshly ground black
   pepper

pinch of dry mustard
3 eggs
milk for binding (optional)
flour for coating
oil or bacon fat (for non-
   vegetarians) for frying

To garnish
sprigs of fresh parsley

1. Mix together the breadcrumbs, leek, cheese, parsley, seasonings and mustard.
2. Beat together 2 eggs and 1 yolk and use this to bind the mixture, adding a little milk if the mixture is too dry to hold together. Divide into 12 portions, form into sausage shapes and roll in flour.
3. Beat the remaining egg white until frothy, brush this over the sausages then coat them in the extra breadcrumbs. Chill for 20 minutes.
4. Fry gently in oil or bacon fat until crisp and golden brown on all sides. Serve immediately, garnished with fresh parsley.

● A spicy tomato chutney is an ideal accompaniment.

M   Not suitable for microwave cookery

F   Freeze individually, spaced out on a tray

AP Prepare up to the end of stage 3

Green salad with honey dressing
Salad gwyrdd gyda mel

I first tasted this salad when touring West Wales and the combination of fresh herbs, honey and mustard made it so outstanding that I suggest you use the dressing with any variety of crisp salad ingredients.

Look in the garden and add a few edible flowers for a change: marigold petals, lavender, violet flowers, clover or nasturtium. All these taste delectable and add great colour to a salad. My thanks to Cnapan guest house in Newport, Pembrokeshire, for this recipe.

1 crisp lettuce – an iceberg,
   Webbs' Wonder or cos
1 bunch watercress
2 tbsp fresh parsley, chopped
2 tbsp fresh chervil, basil or
   sage, chopped
2 tbsp fresh rosemary, thyme
   or savory, chopped
a few edible flowers (optional)

For the honey dressing
6 tbsp best quality olive oil
2 tbsp cider vinegar or lemon
   juice
1 tsp honey
1 tsp wholegrain mustard
salt and freshly ground black
   pepper

1. Rinse and dry all the salad ingredients. Shred the lettuce.
2. In a large salad bowl combine the lettuce with the watercress and freshly chopped herbs. Sprinkle the flowers over the top.
3. Combine all the ingredients for the dressing in a screw-topped jar. Shake well and pour over the salad just before serving. Toss well.

M –

F –

AP Make up the dressing

PUDDINGS

Summer berries with elderflower cream
Sunday rice pudding
Monmouth pudding
Honey, hazelnut and lemon mousse
Honey and ginger syllabub
Gooseberry turnover
Geranium water ice
Dowset
Whisky oatmeal cream
The richest chocolate mousse
Blackcurrant layer pudding
Blackberry crisp
Welsh apple pudding
Apple and ginger fool
Apple pancakes
Berry lemon pudding
Strawberry sethyd
Snowdonia pudding
Welsh bread and butter pudding

'After the plates had been polished clean with bread, the pudding came out, and let me tell you my mother's pudding would make you hold your breath to eat. Sometimes it was a pie or stewed fruit with thick cream from the farm that morning, but whatever it was, it was always good.' Richard Llewellyn in *How Green Was My Valley*.

Traditionally, Welsh puddings have always been based on milk or fruit, so it is not surprising that rice pudding has been the most highly esteemed Sunday pudding for the past century. Besides, when the roast occupies the top half of the oven, how convenient to use the lower, cooler shelf for the rice pud. Ground nutmeg or a bayleaf is sometimes added or even a handful of sultanas for sweetness. Other milk puddings combining breadcrumbs, eggs and butter, such as Snowdonia or Monmouth pudding, are popular in Wales and are creamy-tasting and inexpensive. Junket or curd cakes, using full-fat milk fresh from the cow, are quite delicious, as are pancakes made with buttermilk for a touch of sharpness, and all rich creamy desserts such as syllabubs and fruit fools.

No fools the Welsh when it comes to combing country hedgerows, fields and woodlands for wild fruit and flowers. Blackberry and apple tart, plum crumble, gooseberry pie with elderflower, all these and many more grace the tables of Welsh households. Dried fruits mixed with spices have been enjoyed in Wales ever since the Crusaders returned from the Holy Land, bringing with them such exotic tastes as cinnamon, ginger, apricots, lemons, sultanas and almonds.

If the Welsh housewife's forte lies in baking then she sur-passes herself with pastry. Using the bakestone as the cooking medium, all manner of fruit turnovers are produced with a wonderful short, crisp pastry. Just imagine how dextrous the cook must be to griddle a fruit pie and turn it on a bakestone. The sugar is always added after cooking and this ensures that the pastry stays perfectly crisp.

Again using the bakestone, pancakes are the perfect standby with which to feed unexpected visitors. A combination of flour or oatmeal with fresh milk, eggs and butter, these are always popular, and in Wales currants are often added to sweeten the batter. Spiced apple pancakes with a jug of fresh cream . . . mmm, perfect.

In recent years because of the cut in milk quotas dairy farmers have turned their milk into alternative products and one of these is ice cream. Made with nothing but natural ingredients, flavoured with nuts, fruit or local honey, these creamy ices are heaven to many a hot, weary traveller. Within the last two years a couple of small firms have produced award-winning ice creams and are now distributing them in England. Generally speaking, though, ice cream is rather a local thing and each producer guards their own territory, distributing only within a few hilly miles. Visitors are advised to carry out their own ice-cream survey as they travel through Wales and see which they like best!

Summer berries with elderflower cream
Aeron yr haf gyda hufen blodau'r ysgawen

The idea for this mouthwatering dish was given to me by master chef Chris Chown at his restaurant Plas Bodegroes near Pwllheli in North Wales. After training in London and Switzerland Chris bought this Georgian country house on the Llyn Peninsula to realize his dreams. The locals can't believe their luck – fresh local produce cooked to perfection and all set in the most superb surroundings.

Elderflowers, like so many hedgerow plants, are plentiful in Wales, for much of the countryside is unspoilt. In the past, much use was made of wild fruits and plants, and wine was prepared from a variety of flowers for medicinal purposes. It is still easy to fill baskets with rosehips, sloes, wild strawberries and blackberries if you wander off the beaten track, and elderflowers for this cream should not prove too difficult to find. If, however, you don't have access to a bridlepath or rural hedgerow, then visit the nearest healthfood shop and buy some dried elderflowers instead.

Gather an assortment of summer berries, as many different varieties as you can find. Allow 100 g (4 oz) per person. Prepare and clean them, cook if necessary and place in individual glasses. Chill until needed.

For the elderflower cream
300 ml (½ pint) water
35 g (1½ oz) granulated sugar
3 heads of fresh elderflower,
    picked early in the
    morning, or 25 g (1 oz)
    dried elderflowers

300 ml (10 fl oz) double cream
150 ml (5 fl oz) natural yogurt

To garnish
fresh elderflowers

1. Heat the water in a saucepan and stir in the sugar until it

dissolves. Bring to the boil and boil rapidly for 5 minutes. Take the pan off the heat and submerge the fresh or dried elderflower in this syrup.

2. Leave to infuse for 3 hours then press the syrup through a sieve, discarding the used elderflowers.

3. Whisk the cream until thick, fold in the yogurt and 50 ml (2 fl oz) elderflower syrup and spoon over the chilled fruit. (The remaining syrup can be frozen.)

4. Decorate with fresh elderflowers or any pretty and delicate flowers you may have. Serve with crisp biscuits.

M   Prepare stage 1 in the microwave

F   Not suitable for freezing but you can make a quantity of the elderflower syrup during the summer when the flowers are in season and freeze in small yogurt pots for use during those dreary winter months

AP Make up the syrup in advance

Sunday rice pudding

Pwdin reis dydd sul

The most popular pudding in rural Wales these past 100 years. Traditionally served for Sunday lunch, when aromatic baked rice pudding would follow the roast. A bay leaf and some sweet plump raisins give Welsh rice pudding that little extra which makes it so special.

50 g (2 oz) shortgrain rice   pinch of salt
1 bay leaf   600 ml (1 pint) milk
50 g (2 oz) caster sugar   small knob of butter
50 g (2 oz) raisins or currants   nutmeg, freshly grated

1. Wash the rice and soak in cold water for 15 minutes.
2. Grease a 1.2 l (2 pint) shallow, ovenproof dish, put the bay leaf in and sprinkle in the drained rice. Add the sugar, raisins, salt, milk and butter. Grate the nutmeg over the surface.
3. Cook in a warm oven (gas 3, 325°F, 170°C) for 2–2½ hours, adding a spot more milk if the pudding begins to look dry, until the rice grains are soft and the top is golden brown.

M   For the traditional crisp-baked top to the rice pudding, cook in the conventional oven

F   Freeze well covered, add a little extra milk when reheating

AP Not suitable – reheated rice pudding is never quite the same as one fresh from the oven

Monmouth pudding

Pwdin mynwy

This pudding is regularly on the menu at the Hotel Maes-y-Neuadd near Harlech. Two couples, the Slatters and Horsfalls, run this superb solid mansion house, built out of Welsh granite with a roof of slate. The name translates to 'the mansion in the meadow' and certainly the views are quite breathtaking.

Similar to queen of puddings, this delicious sweet is inexpensive and simple to produce. Originally baked in a large dish, I find that it adapts well to individual servings, and all recipients enjoy having a meringue-covered ramekin to themselves.

grated rind of 1 lemon
2 tbsp caster sugar
25 g (1 oz) butter
450 ml (15 fl oz) milk
175 g (6 oz) fresh white
   breadcrumbs
3 egg yolks

4–5 tsp raspberry jam, or
   100 g (4 oz) fresh seasonal
   fruit – strawberries, cherries
   etc

For the topping
3 egg whites
3 tbsp caster sugar

1. Add the lemon rind, sugar and butter to the milk and bring to the boil. Pour this mixture over the breadcrumbs and leave to stand for 15 minutes.
2. Stir the egg yolks into the cooled bread mixture and spoon into 4 ramekin dishes.
3. Spread a layer of jam or the prepared fresh fruit over the top and cover with the meringue.
4. For the meringue topping: whisk the egg whites till stiff (so stiff that if you turn the bowl upside down they won't fall out), fold in the sugar with a spatula or metal spoon and swirl the meringue on top of the ramekins.

5. Either put the ramekins into a moderately hot oven (gas 6, 400°F, 200°C) for 10 minutes to crisp the meringue (but do watch them carefully) or bake in a slow oven (gas 2–3, 300-325°F, 160–170°C) until the meringue is brown and crisp – about 15 minutes for individual ramekins and 30 minutes for a larger dish.

M   Stage 1 can be prepared in the microwave

F   Not suitable for freezing after stage 2

AP Prepare up to the end of stage 2

Honey, hazelnut and lemon mousse
Mousse o fêl, cnau cyll a lemwn

The Meadowsweet Hotel in Llanrwst, North Wales, first introduced me to this superb mousse. The recipe calls for a fair amount of patience and concentration but the final result is worth it.

3 tbsp top quality runny honey
juice of 1 lemon
75 g (3 oz) hazelnuts, finely chopped
2 egg yolks
3 eggs
50 g (2 oz) caster sugar

150 ml (5 fl oz) double cream
12 g (½ oz) gelatine
2 tbsp mead or sweet sherry

To garnish
whipped cream
hazelnuts

1. Mix the honey, lemon juice and hazelnuts together.
2. Put the egg yolks and whole eggs in a basin with the caster sugar and whisk over gentle heat (sit the basin on top of a saucepan of hot water) until thick and mousse-like.
3. Once thick, cool the mousse as quickly as possible. The best method is to place the bowl in a larger bowl which has been filled with ice cubes or iced water. Then fold in the honey, nuts and lemon juice. Whisk the cream until thick and fold it into the mousse.
4. Dissolve the gelatine in the mead or sherry (see p. 22) then pour this into the mousse, stirring gently in a continuous movement to distribute the gelatine evenly. Don't stir too hard or you will knock the lightness out of the mousse.
5. As the mousse begins to set, pour it into a serving bowl or individual dishes. Chill for an hour. Garnish with a dollop of cream topped with a whole hazelnut.

M   Not suitable for microwave cookery

F   Can be frozen for a short while, say, up to a week, but cover well to stop a leathery skin forming on top

AP Prepare up to 8 hours in advance, chill in the fridge until required

Honey and ginger syllabub

Syllabub mel a sinsir

A real winner this one. Lovely, as the Welsh say. Ginger has been a favourite in Wales for centuries. Traditionally it is used to add flavour to cakes, homemade wines, even fish, so it's hardly surprising to find this bewitching combination of ginger, honey and wine here in the principality.

2 tbsp clear Welsh honey
300 ml (10 fl oz) double cream
300 ml (10 fl oz) sweet white
  wine (elderberry is
  delicious)
50 g (2 oz) stem or crystalized
  ginger, finely chopped

To garnish
4 chunks ginger
sugared mint leaves (see
  p. 45)

1. Place the honey and cream in a bowl. Gradually add the wine, whisking continuously to a light foam.
2. Fold in the chopped ginger and pour into tall stemmed glasses.
3. Chill slightly, then decorate with the extra ginger and sugared mint leaves.
• Serve with fingers of shortbread or crisp, thin dessert biscuits.

M –

F Not suitable for freezing

AP This takes only minutes to whisk together, so prepare no more than 2 hours in advance in case it separates

Gooseberry turnover

Tarten planc eirin mair

A traditional dish from Wales which is cooked on a bakestone or planc. This fruit tart is prepared like a Cornish pasty but instead of being baked in the oven it is cooked first on one side and then the other on a griddle. Not an easy trick to perform, turning your tart, but there are many dextrous Welsh housewives who remember back to those times when the bakestone, together with the stew pot, was the main method of cooking in Wales. Watch out that the pastry doesn't break when you turn it over, or the fruit will leak out and burn the surface of the griddle. For ease, I suggest that you prepare individual turnovers. Rhubarb could be substituted for gooseberries if you prefer. My thanks to Eleri Davies for this recipe.

Makes 6 small turnovers or 1 large

For the shortcrust pastry
75 g (3 oz) plain white flour
75 g (3 oz) stoneground
   brown flour
75 g (3 oz) butter
pinch of salt
water to mix

For the filling
450 g (1 lb) gooseberries,
   topped and tailed
1 head of elderflower
sugar to taste

1. Make the pastry by sifting the two flours into a bowl then rubbing in the butter until the mixture resembles fine breadcrumbs. Add the salt and enough water to make a firm dough then chill for 30 minutes.
2. Meanwhile, cook the gooseberries in a minimum of water together with the elderflower. Add sugar to taste and leave to cool.
3. Roll the pastry out to 0.5 cm (¼ in) thick and cut into rounds

with a 7.5 cm (3 in) pastry cutter. Put 1 tbsp of gooseberries on half of the discs, brush the edges with milk and cover each with another circle of pastry. Seal the edges well and bake over a moderate heat on a lightly greased griddle or frying pan, turning carefully to cook both sides.

- Serve while still warm, dredged with caster sugar and accompanied by a bowl of cream.

M   Prepare the gooseberries in the microwave

F   Excellent for freezing

AP Make in advance, reheat in a low oven

Geranium water ice

Ia mynawyd y bugail

I first came across this delicate and delicious idea while touring North Wales. It is just the type of fresh flavour that Brigid and Peter Kindred serve their guests at Tyddyn Llan Country House Hotel. Using local produce wherever possible, Brigid feeds her guests wonderfully well after their relaxing day spent walking, bird watching, fishing or sailing in the vicinity.

Rose geranium leaves give this water ice a fragrant and delicate flavour, perfect for a warm summer's evening. Mint and marjoram leaves can be used in exactly the same manner, and also make delicious water ices. Remember that the flavour and texture improve if you take the water ice out of the freezer in plenty of time so that it can soften slightly.

10 rose geranium leaves
300 ml (½ pint) water
50 g (2 oz) granulated sugar
a few drops of rose water
1 egg white

To garnish
rose geranium flowers

1. Boil the geranium leaves in the water for 10 minutes. Remove the leaves, add the sugar and stir to dissolve.
2. Cool this sugar syrup then pour into a plastic container and freeze until ice crystals form round the sides of the bowl.
3. Take out of the freezer and, using a hand or electric whisk, beat well, so that it becomes light and fluffy, adding rose water to strengthen the flavour.
4. Whisk the egg white until thick and frothy, fold into the water ice and freeze again.
5. Half an hour before serving, transfer the water ice to the fridge to allow it to soften a little.

6. Serve spoonfuls of the water ice in wine glasses. Garnish with rose geranium flowers placed on the saucers.

M   Prepare stage 1 in the microwave

F   Both the flavour and texture deteriorate if left in the freezer for more than a week

AP   Make a day or two in advance and leave in the freezer until an hour before serving

Dowset

In her authoritative book *Welsh Fare*, Minwel Tibbott suggests that this pudding was baked in the wall oven by farmers' wives living in the Gower region of West Glamorgan.

It is a baked custard cooked in a pastry shell, and I think that the basic recipe benefits from some additional flavouring. You could use some jam, marmalade or even honey spread over the pastry base or, as I have done here, flavour the custard with some fragrant edible flowers.

For the pastry
175 g (6 oz) flour
75 g (3 oz) butter
3–4 tbsp cold water
pinch of salt

For the filling
2 large eggs

1 dsp flour
300 ml (½ pint) milk
2 tbsp sugar
1 tsp grated nutmeg or 1 tsp chopped edible flowers: either elderflower, violet, marigold or clover

1. Make up the pastry (see Katt pie, p. 191). Chill for a couple of hours then roll out and use to line a 23 cm (9 in) shallow ovenproof dish or plate.
2. Beat the eggs together, whisk in the flour and add the milk gradually to make a batter.
3. Stir in the sugar and flowers or nutmeg and pour into the pastry case. Bake in a moderately hot oven (gas 5, 375°F, 190°C) for about 30 minutes or until set.
• Serve on its own or perhaps with a bowl of summer fruits such as strawberries or raspberries.

M   To achieve the delicate colour and texture required for
    Dowset I recommend that it is cooked in the conventional
    oven

F   Not suitable for freezing

AP Make in advance. Reheat in a very low oven to serve

Whisky oatmeal cream
Blawd ceirch gyda wisgi a hufen

Borrowed from the Scots, I hear you say, this combination of whisky and oatmeal is a flummery . . . But did you know that the English word flummery is derived from the Welsh *llymru*?

Oatmeal has long been a staple of the Welsh diet and whisky is equally famed for its place in Welsh history. Originally created on Bardsey Island, just off the Pembroke coast, it has been made in various places throughout Wales from the 4th century A.D. to the early 20th century when the last distillery, at Bala, closed in response to the demands of the temperance movement. But Welsh whisky lives on, and today the Brecon Brewery under the skilful eye of Dafydd Gittins produces Welsh *wisgi* under the name *Swn y Mor* (Sound of the Sea).

4 tbsp medium oatmeal
3–4 tbsp whisky
2 tbsp heather honey
1 tbsp lemon juice
150 ml (5 fl oz) double cream

To garnish
sprigs of purple heather

1. First toast the oatmeal to give this pudding a really nutty flavour. Either spread it out on a baking sheet and toast for a few minutes under the grill or in a hot oven, or spread evenly over a plate and bake in the microwave until golden brown. Leave to cool.
2. In a small jug mix together the whisky, honey and lemon juice.
3. Whisk the cream until thick but not stiff, then gradually pour in the whisky, honey and lemon mixture, maintaining the thickness of the cream by hard whisking.

4. Fold in the toasted oatmeal and spoon the mixture into tall, stemmed glasses. Chill until needed.
5. Serve the glasses on saucers on each of which there is a sprig of heather.

M   Prepare stage 1 in the microwave

F   Not suitable for freezing

AP Prepare up to the end of stage 2

The richest chocolate mousse
Mousse siocled cyfoethog

There's no denying the fact that we all love chocolate. Ever since the Spaniards brought it to Europe in 1519 from Mexico we've been addicted. Brillat-Savarin declared it was one of the most effective restoratives – and isn't it true how a bar of chocolate can lift the spirits? As a stimulant it has superb qualities, although in Wales some have come to regret this. To quote from the *Llanelli Mercury*, 'By the use of chocolate my wife has been brought to bed of twins three times.'!

225 g (8 oz) best quality plain chocolate, such as Bournville
300 ml (10 fl oz) single cream

1 egg
1 tbsp brandy – or to taste

1. Grate the chocolate coarsely and add to the cream in a saucepan. Heat gently until the chocolate has melted but don't let the cream boil.
2. Pour into a liquidizer, add the egg and brandy and blend until smooth and creamy.
3. Pour the chocolate mousse into little pots or ramekins and leave to set for 3 hours or overnight.
- This is very rich and I suggest that you serve plain crisp biscuits with it. A dollop of whipped cream looks pretty on top or you can leave it quite plain.

M   Heat with care in the microwave

F   Not suitable for freezing

AP Make the day before

Blackcurrant layer pudding

Pwdin haenog cwrens duon

A midsummer pudding, simplicity itself, with a crunchy taste and good blend of flavours. The sharpness of the blackcurrants contrasts well with the honey, nut and breadcrumb layer. Make this pudding a few hours in advance and leave in the fridge for a while to allow the tastes to mellow.

450 g (1 lb) freshly picked
   blackcurrants
150 ml (¼ pint) water
grated rind and juice of 1
   orange
1 tbsp honey
225 g (8 oz) wholemeal
   breadcrumbs

25 g (1 oz) dessicated coconut
50 g (2 oz) hazelnuts,
   chopped
50 g (2 oz) demerara sugar

To garnish
chopped nuts
slices of fresh orange

1. Top and tail the blackcurrants then stew them gently in a saucepan with the water, orange rind and juice. Sweeten with the honey and leave to cool.
2. Spread the breadcrumbs over a large baking tray and toast or bake in a moderate oven (gas 4, 350°F, 180°C) for 20 minutes until crisp and golden. Cool, then mix with the coconut, hazelnuts and sugar.
3. In a large glass bowl or four tall, stemmed glasses layer the dry ingredients with the blackcurrants. Garnish with chopped nuts and slices of orange. Serve with plain yogurt or cream.

M   Cook the fruit in the microwave

F   Freeze the stewed fruit mixture but not the complete pudding

AP Prepare up to six hours in advance

Blackberry crisp
Mwyar duon gyda briwsion bara

A real hedgerow pudding this, and all the more delicious for it. To a poor mining family freshly picked blackberries must have been like manna from heaven, adding a taste of luxury for free.

'O, blackberry tart, with berries as big as your thumb, purple and black, and thick with juice, and a crust to endear them that will go to cream in your mouth, and both passing down with such a taste that will make you close your eyes and wish you might live for ever in the wideness of that rich moment.' Richard Llewellyn in *How Green Was My Valley*.

Serves 6

175 g (6 oz) wholemeal
  breadcrumbs
675 g (1½ lb) blackberries,
  fresh if possible but frozen
  will do
2 large bananas, sliced

225 g (8 oz) soft brown sugar
50 g (2 oz) butter or
  margarine
juice and grated rind of 2
  oranges

1. Sprinkle 50 g (2 oz) of the breadcrumbs over the bottom of a greased 1.7 l (3 pint) dish. Cover with the blackberries and banana slices and then sprinkle over the remaining crumbs.
2. Put the sugar, butter, grated orange rind and juice in a saucepan and heat together gently until the sugar has dissolved.
3. Pour the sauce over the pudding and bake in a hot oven (gas 6, 400°F, 200°C) for about 30 minutes until crisp and golden brown.
• Serve hot or cold with cream or custard.

M Cook in the microwave, finish under the grill

F Not suitable; the breadcrumbs will become very soggy

AP Prepare up to the end of stage 2

Welsh apple pudding
Pwdin afal cymreig

There is a Welsh myth in which King Curio's soul is hidden in an apple which itself is hidden in the stomach of a salmon, this fish coming to light only once in seven years.

Here is the recipe for a traditional Welsh apple pudding which is as popular now as it ever was. Bowls of steaming pudding might well have been served to hungry harvesters at the end of a busy day in the fields. Supper was taken out to them on large trays, hearty meals full of goodness.

450 g (1 lb) cooking apples,
   peeled, cored and sliced
4 tbsp water
100 g (4 oz) granulated sugar
4 cloves
35 g (1½ oz) butter

50 g (2 oz) flour
450 ml (¾ pint) milk
25 g (1 oz) caster sugar
2 eggs, separated
few drops vanilla essence

1. In a saucepan cook the apples with the water, granulated sugar and cloves until tender. Remove cloves and place the apple in a well-buttered ovenproof dish.
2. Melt the butter in a saucepan, stir in the flour and gradually add the milk. Bring slowly to the boil, stirring constantly. Remove from the heat, add the caster sugar, egg yolks and vanilla essence, and mix thoroughly.
3. Whisk the egg whites until stiff. Fold into the sauce and pour it over the apples. Bake for 45 minutes in a moderately hot oven (gas 5–6, 375–400°F, 190–200°C) until risen and crisp all over.
- Serve hot with pouring cream, ice cream or natural yogurt mixed with a little honey.

M   Cook the apples in the microwave, and also the sauce until
    the egg yolks are added

F   Freeze the apple base but not the topping

AP Prepare and cook the apples and the sauce, but don't fold
    in the egg whites until the last minute

Apple and ginger fool
Pwdin afal a sinsir

Richard Llewellyn writes in *How Green Was My Valley*, 'I often think of apple and ginger fool, and plum pie and medlar trifle.' A fool is such a simple dish. But take care not to drown the flavours of the fruit with too much cream as is often the case, or even by the addition of too much custard in a 'school dinner'-type fool. The perfect fool should be a blend of fruit and cream in proportions that enhance the flavour of the fruit.

675 g (1½ lb) cooking apples, peeled, cored and chopped
25 g (1 oz) fresh root ginger, peeled and grated, or a 2.5 cm (1 in) knob of crystalized or stem ginger, finely chopped
3 cloves

1 tbsp honey
300 ml (10 fl oz) double cream, lightly whipped

To garnish
slivers of stem or crystalized ginger, or grated nutmeg

1. Cook the apples very gently with the ginger and cloves in a minimum of water. Stir in the honey to taste, and cool.
2. Remove the cloves. Mash the apples with a fork to make a purée.
3. With a large metal spoon carefully fold the apple purée into the whipped cream without completely combining the two, so that it has a marbled look. Spoon into tall, stemmed glasses and garnish with a few slivers of stem or crystalized ginger or a sprinkling of grated nutmeg.
• Serve with crisp, thin ginger biscuits.

M   Cook the apples in the microwave

F   Freeze in one large serving dish

AP Make up the fool a few hours in advance and chill in the fridge. Garnish at the last moment

Apple pancakes
Crempogau afal

Crempog, or pancakes, could almost become the national dish of Wales, so popular are they. Look in any bakery in Wales and you will see at least one of the many varieties of pancake. On the whole they are thick, sweet and filled with currants; some include a raising agent such as baking powder, and many are made with buttermilk. In Swansea market you can queue by the baker's stall and eat one straight from the griddle. This recipe combines pancakes with caramelized apple – a better combination would be hard to find.

For the batter
300 ml (½ pint) milk + 1 tbsp
   water
2 eggs
1 tbsp butter, melted
100 g (4 oz) flour

For the filling
50 g (2 oz) butter
50 g (2 oz) soft brown sugar
450 g (1 lb) cooking apples,
   peeled, cored and chopped
a good pinch of mixed spice
brandy to taste
icing sugar to glaze

1. First prepare the batter: put all the ingredients in a liquidizer and whizz until smooth. Leave for 30 minutes to thicken.
2. For the filling: in a medium saucepan melt the butter gently, then add the sugar and continue to cook until the sugar has dissolved. Turn the heat up and allow the butter and sugar to caramelize, i.e. turn a rich brown colour, but on no account let them burn and blacken.
3. Tip the apples into the saucepan and cook gently until soft. Add the spice and brandy and leave to cool.
4. Fry the pancakes, as thinly as possible in a shallow frying pan (see p. 21).

5. Put some apple mixture on each pancake, fold or roll them and place in a heatproof dish. Reheat gently under the grill for 5 minutes then dust with icing sugar and pop under a very hot grill to glaze.

● Serve at once with cream, sour cream, yogurt or a mixture of any.

M   Not suitable for microwave cookery

F   Freeze the pancakes well wrapped in a polythene bag. Allow to thaw completely before separating

AP Prepare and fill the pancakes. When required, reheat under a warm grill for 5 minutes before turning the heat up to glaze them

Berry lemon pudding

Pwdin aeron a lemwn

Whinberries (bilberries) give this dish a very special Welsh flavour. They grow during the late summer months on wild heathland or in hedgerows and look similar to American blueberries but smaller. If you manage to find some growing wild then pick as many as you can. They add a marvellous flavour to any 'berry' pudding. Blackberries, or any fresh summer fruit from raspberries to apricots, will make a good substitute if whinberries elude you.

225 g (½ lb) whinberries, or any fresh fruit you have to hand
25 g (1 oz) unsalted butter
100 g (4 oz) soft brown sugar
grated rind and juice of 1 lemon
25 g (1 oz) flour
2 eggs, separated
150 ml (¼ pint) milk

1. Prepare the fruit: wash and hull the berries, set a few aside for decoration and put the rest into a 600 ml (1 pint) soufflé dish.
2. In a large bowl cream together the butter with half of the sugar. Add the grated lemon rind then add alternately, beating hard between each addition, the remaining sugar, the flour, egg yolks and milk.
3. Whisk the egg whites till stiff and fold them into the mixture. Pour on to the fruit and sit the soufflé dish in a baking tin containing 2.5 cm (1 in) of water.
4. Cook in a moderate oven (gas 4, 350°F, 180°C) for 45 minutes until the top is brown and spongy.
• Either serve hot dredged with caster sugar or cold with a decoration of piped cream and the remaining berries.

M   This pudding can be cooked in the microwave but crisp
    under a hot grill just before serving to add some colour to
    the sponge

F   Not suitable for freezing

AP Prepare the fruit and put ready in the soufflé dish. Make
    up and add the sponge to cook when required

Strawberry sethyd

Sethyd mefys

Henry VIII so enjoyed his puddings that it was not unthinkable for him to reward the inventor of a successful new recipe with an extravagant gift, say a small manor house! One of his favourite recipes was strawberries soaked or seethed overnight in claret and sweetened with honey and woodruff. Serve with cream.

450 g (1 lb) fresh,
  unblemished strawberries
300 ml (10 fl oz) claret (a
  lesser red wine will suffice)
1 tbsp runny honey
1 good sprig woodruff (or
  substitute fresh orange mint
  or lemon mint)

To serve
a large bowl of whipped
  cream, or if you prefer a
  tangy touch, blend an equal
  quantity of natural yogurt
  with whipped cream

1. Hull the strawberries, wash quickly if muddy. Put them in a deep bowl, taking care not to bruise them.
2. Stir the honey and woodruff into the wine and pour over the strawberries.
3. Seethe (macerate) the fruit in the wine overnight in a cool place.
4. Serve the strawberries just as they are with the bowl of cream.
• A plate of shell shortbread (see p. 295) would add a crisp bite to this delicious dessert.

M –

F Not suitable for freezing

AP Prepare the strawberries the day before

Snowdonia pudding
Pwdin eryri

As the name suggests, this suet pudding was created in the beautiful mountain range of Snowdon. John Ellis Roberts, head warden with the National Park, says that the Pen-y-Gwrwd Hotel at the foot of Snowdonia still prepares this tasty and substantial pudding for its energetic guests, to sustain them while walking over the mountains.

100 g (4 oz) suet (animal or
   vegetarian)
100 g (4 oz) fresh white
   breadcrumbs
25 g (1 oz) cornflour or
   ground rice
pinch of salt
75 g (3 oz) demerara sugar
grated rind of 1 lemon
50 g (2 oz) raisins
3 eggs
75 g (3 oz) lemon or orange
   marmalade

For the wine sauce
75 g (3 oz) granulated sugar
150 ml (¼ pint) water
grated rind of 1 lemon
25 g (1 oz) butter
1 tbsp flour
100 ml (4 fl oz) Madeira,
   sherry or white wine
a good pinch of nutmeg

1. Mix the suet, breadcrumbs, cornflour, salt, demerara sugar and grated lemon rind together. Grease a 1.2 l (2 pint) basin and press about half of the raisins on to the greased sides.
2. Beat the eggs with the marmalade and add to the dry ingredients with the remaining raisins.
3. Pour into the basin, cover with a pleated sheet of greaseproof paper (the pleat allows the pudding to swell a little) and boil for 1½ hours in a saucepan half filled with water. (A gentle

simmer is enough to cook the pudding, but on no account let the pan boil dry.)

4. For the wine sauce: in a saucepan, dissolve the sugar in the water over gentle heat, add the lemon rind and simmer for 10 minutes. Strain and cool.

5. Melt the butter, stir in the flour and pour in the sugar syrup. Add the Madeira, sherry or white wine and simmer for 5 minutes. Stir in the nutmeg.

6. Serve the pudding turned out on to a large serving plate with the sauce poured over.

M   Cooks well in the microwave

F   Freeze in the bowl if possible or well wrapped in slices. Don't freeze the sauce

AP Remember to put the pudding on to cook in time for dinner! Suet puddings must be eaten freshly made

Welsh bread and butter pudding
Pwdin bara cymreig

One dark, dank, dreary November evening I found myself dining at the Stables Hotel in Llangattock, not far from Brecon in Powys. The welcome was warm and as we settled ourselves in front of the enormous fire, taking in the plethora of hunting scenes and trophies around us, promising smells began to waft in from the kitchen. We were not disappointed and all that we ate was good, but none better than this bread and butter pudding. It really is the best I have ever eaten and I must thank Penelope's mother who so kindly divulged the recipe to me.

3 slices medium-sliced white bread, decrusted and cut into cubes

2 tbsp demerara sugar

50 g (2 oz) butter, cut into lumps

a large handful of mixed dried fruit

juice and grated rind of 1 orange

3 new-laid eggs

600 ml (1 pint) milk

½ tsp powdered cinnamon or mixed spice

1. Arrange the cubes of bread in a shallow ovenproof dish. Sprinkle over the sugar, butter, fruit, grated orange rind and orange juice.
2. Beat the eggs together with a fork, stir in the milk and pour over the pudding. Dust with the powdered spice.
3. Put the dish into a baking tin containing 2.5 cm (1 in) water and bake for one hour in a moderately hot oven (gas 5, 375°F, 190°C).

M   Suitable for microwave cookery

F   Not suitable for freezing

AP Prepare and cook in advance. Reheat in a *bain-marie* (see p. 21)

BAKING

Carrot cake
Anglesey cake
Welsh cakes
Tinker's cakes
Bara Brith
Pikelets
Honey buns
Gingerbread
Wholemeal sponge
Teisen Lap
Stoneground wholemeal bread
Shell shortbread
Farmhouse oatcakes
Llanddarog Fair cakes
Honey and ginger cake
Caerphilly scones
Buttermilk bread
Crunchy bran fingers
Apple cake

During the rugger season Cardiff sways to the music coming out of Arms Park, and what are those crowds singing? 'Bread of Heaven'. The Welsh are proud of their bread and rightly so for there has always been a fine tradition of baking in Wales. From our Celtic ancestors we have learnt how to griddle, bake with oats and make a loaf so good that it was thought of not as the mainstay to a frugal diet but rather as a luxury. Richard Llewellyn, brought up in the mining valleys of South Wales at the beginning of this century, waxes lyrical about bread: 'There is a good dripping toast in by the fire in the evening. Good jelly dripping and crusty, home-baked bread, with the mealy savour of ripe wheat roundly in your mouth and under your teeth, roasted sweet and crisp and deep brown, and covered with little pockets where the dripping will hide and melt and shine in the light, deep down inside, ready to run when your teeth bite it. Butter is good too, mind. But I will have my butter with plain bread and butter, cut in the long slice, and I will say of its kind, there is nothing you will have better, especially if the butter is an hour out of the churn and spread tidy.'

You can imagine the industry in the farmhouse kitchen on baking day from morn till night, with the oven lit specially to bake bread, scones, fruit breads and such like. That delicious smell of freshly baked bread would fill the house, and yes, there was always homemade butter to spread on it, not to mention jam made from hedgerow pickings, and farmhouse cheese. Wonderful!

Travelling round Wales you will find many regional speciali-ties, some of which appear in this book – Welsh cakes, Bara

Brith, malt breads, tea cakes, Teisen Lap, caraway loaves, pudding cake, honey bread, buttermilk bread, gingerbread, Bara Gwenith, bakestones, pikelets, Anglesey cake, Swansea loaves and even the Towyn butter bun. If these are the traditional bakery items then there is also a whole new range of fashionable bread – granary, wholemeal, stoneground, sesame, pitta, seed bread, and the like. And the ease with which these breads are made in Wales stems from the quality, stoneground flours produced in a handful of renovated water mills. Given the combination of a good Welsh baker and stoneground flours full of goodness and tasty grain it's no wonder that Welsh bread is good.

Oats, again a modern favourite – think of muesli and flapjacks – are found often on Welsh menus. In the past, oats were used to thicken soups and stews, or combined with buttermilk in pancakes, but the most common recipe for oats was the Welsh oatcake. Similiar to Scottish oatcakes but usually thinner and sometimes a great deal wider, these crisp, tasty biscuits are still cooked on a bakestone. Lady Llanover, writing *Good Cookery* in 1867, says 'the preparation of oatmeal is particularly well understood in Wales, as well as in Scotland. Next to bread and good water, oatmeal may be considered as one of the first necessities of life to a rural population, indeed, in some parts of Wales, it still takes the place of bread in many instances; the Welsh render it to them almost as a staff of life.'

The bakestone, planc or maen as it is known in various regions of Wales still plays an important part in everyday life. Imagine the Celtic kitchen, with the hearth full of hot embers, the family gathered round and a bakestone sizzling with scones or pancakes. Today we have microwave ovens, electric fan ovens, gas and Calor gas ovens, but none griddle as does the sustained, deep, dry heat of a bakestone. A great deal of patience as well as experience is needed when cooking, say, a loaf of bread on a bakestone, to ensure that the middle cooks through without burning the outer crust.

To emphasize the significance of good bread to the Welsh, let me finish with this quotation from David Parry-Jones in his book *Welsh Country Upbringing*: 'When there was an illness in the family, folks came from miles around to get a loaf or two of

Morgans' bread. Expectant mothers were given Morgans' loaves by their husbands. I verily believe that many mothers' labour was forgotten in the anticipation of the joy that it would be to live for a few days on Morgans' bread!'

Carrot cake

Teisen foron

No, I can't claim that carrots are singular to Wales, but there is something in the simplicity of this recipe that blends with Welsh cooking. The moist nuttiness of this cake is very moreish, and a slice cut just as soon as it comes out of the oven will claim even the most ardent weight watcher!

175 g (6 oz) butter or firm margarine
225 g (8 oz) caster sugar
2 eggs, beaten
225 g (8 oz) self-raising flour

2 tsp cinnamon or mixed spice
pinch of salt
225 g (8 oz) raw carrot, grated
100 g (4 oz) walnuts, chopped

1. Cream the butter with the sugar until very soft and light in texture and colour. (This always takes longer than you think, but allow at least 5 minutes.) Beat in the eggs, one at a time.
2. Sieve together the flour, spice and salt and fold them into the creamed mixture with a large metal spoon. Fold in the carrots and nuts and turn the mixture at once into a greased and lined 900 g (2 lb) loaf tin or 20 cm (8 in) deep cake tin.
3. Bake in a moderate oven (gas 4, 350°F, 180°C) for 1¼ hours until cooked right through and crisp and golden on the top. (To test, stick a skewer into the middle of the cake and if it comes out quite clean without any sticky cake mixture on it, then the cake is done.) Turn out on to a wire tray to cool.
• Serve freshly baked; if it is a day or two old spread butter or cream cheese over the slices.

M   Suitable for microwave cookery

F   Freeze whole or in slices for easy thawing

Anglesey cake
Cacen sir fon

In the middle of the 18th century when treacle was much cheaper to buy than refined sugar it was often used to sweeten porridge and puddings. In Wales – and the island of Anglesey in particular – treacle was added to cakes to give them an appearance of richness. Anglesey cakes, darkened with treacle, were often served at weddings by families too poor to afford wedding cakes. Today the cake survives as a moist, dark-brown delicacy – with the recipe, sometimes known as 'granny's recipe', being handed down from generation to generation.

100 g (4 oz) butter
75 g (3 oz) soft brown sugar
1 egg, beaten
1 tbsp black treacle
275 g (10 oz) self-raising flour
½ tsp salt

1 tsp ground ginger
1 tsp mixed spice
½ tsp bicarbonate of soda
200 ml (7 fl oz) milk
175 g (6 oz) mixed dried fruit

1. Cream the butter and sugar until pale and fluffy. Beat in the egg and mix in the treacle.
2. Sieve together the flour, salt, ginger and mixed spice and stir into the creamed mixture.
3. Dissolve the bicarbonate of soda in the milk, add gradually to the mixture and stir thoroughly before adding the dried fruit.
4. Spoon into a greased and lined 20 cm (8 in) round cake tin and bake in a warm oven (gas 3, 325°F, 170°C) for 50–60 minutes, or until a skewer inserted in the centre of the cake comes out clean.

• The cake is best kept for 24 hours before cutting, and keeps well in an airtight tin.

M   Suitable for microwave cookery

F   Freeze well wrapped, whole or in slices

Welsh cakes

Picau ar y maen/cacennau cri

These little cakes are cooked on a griddle and you can see them being baked in the traditional manner in Swansea market every day of the week. Although all the Celtic countries use the bakestone it is only the Welsh who griddle these scone-like buns. Recipes for Welsh cakes are manifold, but this is the one I favour for its dry-baked outside, moist texture and spicy flavour. A heavy saucepan or skillet will serve as a griddle or bakestone.

Makes approx 24

175 g (6 oz) lard and butter
   mixed
450 g (1 lb) self-raising flour
175 g (6 oz) caster sugar
1 tsp baking powder

½ tsp mixed spice
75 g (3 oz) sultanas or
   currants
2 eggs, beaten

1. Rub the fat into the flour, then stir in the sugar, baking powder, spice and sultanas. Add the eggs and mix to a firm dough.
2. On a lightly floured board roll out the dough and stamp into 5 cm (2 in) circles using a pastry cutter.
3. Griddle very gently on a lightly greased pan or bakestone for about 3–4 minutes each side. Welsh cakes burn very easily so keep the heat low to allow the middle to cook through.
4. Dust with caster sugar and eat immediately or store in an airtight tin.

M   Not suitable for microwave cookery

F   Perfect for freezing. Cover well. Welsh cakes thaw in minutes

Tinker's cakes

Teisennau tincer

It's a romantic idea to think that these tasty little griddle cakes were made specially for travelling tinkers. Were they made in anticipation of a call or in celebration of the tinker's arrival? Or indeed, did he always carry a pocketful!

Makes 10

225 g (8 oz) flour   ½ tsp cinnamon
pinch of salt   1 medium cooking apple
100 g (4 oz) butter   1 tbsp milk (optional)
75 g (3 oz) soft brown sugar

1. Sieve the flour and salt into a large bowl and rub in the butter until the mixture resembles fine breadcrumbs. Add the sugar and cinnamon.
2. Peel the apple then grate it straight into the mixture, stirring to stop any brown colour forming. Add the milk only if the mixture won't hold together to make a firm dough when pressed with your hands.
3. Turn on to a floured board and roll or pat out to about 0.5 cm (¼ in) thick. Either cut into 5 cm (2 in) rounds with a pastry cutter or shape into larger, 10 cm (4 in) circles (more difficult to deal with but more fun to serve).
4. To prepare the griddle or heavy-based frying pan, pour a tsp of oil on to a piece of kitchen paper, rub this over the cooking area and don't add any more oil unless the cakes stick. Cook the Tinker's cakes gently for about 3 minutes on each side.
5.. Serve warm from the griddle, well sprinkled with caster sugar. Cut the larger discs into wedges.

M   Not suitable for microwave cookery

F   Excellent for freezing, seal in bags or plastic boxes. Reheat
gently in the oven

Bara Brith

This is literally translated as speckled bread. Once a week the stove was lit for baking day and from dawn to dusk the smell of fresh bread wafted out of the kitchen. As the heat began to fade in the stove so a handful of currants was added to the last of the bread dough and this speckled bread became a treat. Bara Brith is no more than a fatless fruit loaf, prepared in most parts of the British Isles under another name. The flavour, however, of this spiced, honey-glazed fruit bread is delicious when spread with salted Welsh butter, and it is no wonder that Bara Brith is still produced all over Wales. This is not a traditional recipe but one that I have used for years and which is simple and successful.

450 g (1 lb) mixed dried fruit
300 ml (½ pint) tea
2 tbsp marmalade
1 egg, beaten

6 tbsp soft brown sugar
1 tsp mixed spice
450 g (1 lb) self-raising flour
honey to glaze

1. Soak the fruit overnight in the tea.
2. Next day, mix in the marmalade, egg, sugar, spice and flour. Spoon into a greased 900 g (1 lb) loaf tin and bake in a warm oven (gas 3, 325°F, 170°C) for 1¾ hours or until the centre is cooked through. Check from time to time that the top doesn't brown too much, and cover with a sheet of foil or move down a shelf in the oven if necessary.
3. Once cooked, leave the Bara Brith to stand for 5 minutes then tip out of the tin on to a cooling tray. Using a pastry brush, glaze the top with honey.
• Serve sliced with salted butter and some tasty farmhouse Cheddar. Store in an airtight tin.

M   May be cooked in the microwave but the firm texture and
    lovely colour are somewhat lost

F   Freeze wrapped in foil, whole or in slices

Pikelets

Pice'r pregethwr

'On butter-making days, the house resounded to the noise of continuous clap, clap, clap . . . one of those pleasant sounds that have disappeared, never again to return.' *Welsh Country Upbringing* by David Parry-Jones.

And what more could one ask for than lashings of butter spread over these scrumptious pikelets or drop scones, with perhaps a dollop of homemade jam!

300 ml (½ pint) milk
2 eggs
75 g (3 oz) butter, melted

100 g (4 oz) flour
2 tbsp currants, sultanas or
   raisins (optional)

1. Pour the milk into a liquidizer. Add the eggs, melted butter and flour. Blend to a smooth batter then add the currants if you wish to include them. Leave to stand for 30 minutes.
2. Heat and lightly grease a griddle or heavy-based frying pan and bake one large ladleful or small cupful of the batter at a time until bubbles appear on the surface, then turn over and cook for another minute.
3. Serve hot and buttered with a sprinkling of sugar on top.
- For a change, make up some savoury pikelets by adding 50 g (2 oz) grated Cheddar cheese and some snippets of ham or crisp bacon to the batter. These make an ideal snack for high tea.

M   Not suitable for microwave cookery

F   Freezes extremely well. Toast or grill from frozen to reheat

Honey buns

Byns mel

Teatime in Wales is a very special occasion, for the Welsh are fine bakers. To quote from *How Green Was My Valley* by Richard Llewellyn, whose upbringing in a coal-mining valley was very much dominated by food: 'In a moment the kitchen was full. All the girls ran round the back lane and through the back door, and processions came and went through the front, all taking out plates of bread and butter and pies and cakes and buckets and baths of hot water for the tea pots, all getting in each other's way and laughing and pushing and pretending to be stuck in the doorway.'

These little honey buns are sweet and delicious and make ideal picnic and family food.

100 g (4 oz) butter
100 g (4 oz) soft brown sugar
1 egg, separated
100 ml (4 fl oz) honey
225 g (8 oz) flour

½ tsp bicarbonate of soda
½ tsp cinnamon
1–2 tbsp milk
caster sugar to dredge

1. Cream the butter and sugar together until light and fluffy – this process is important and the longer you beat the better the cakes will be. Add the egg yolk and honey.
2. Sieve together the flour, bicarbonate of soda and cinnamon and fold into the mixture, adding enough milk to moisten if very stiff. Whisk the egg white until stiff and fold in.
3. Divide the mixture between greased bun tins and dust with caster sugar. Bake in a hot oven (gas 7, 425°F, 220°C) for about 20 minutes, until well risen and firm to the touch.

M I find baking small buns in the microwave a fiddly business, as only a few can be cooked at a time. It is better to use the conventional oven and bake a couple of trays at once

F These honey buns freeze well. Pop them in a polythene bag as soon as they are cool and freeze at once

Gingerbread

Bara sinsir

Thumbing through books of traditional Welsh recipes I have three times come across a recipe for gingerbread that has, alas, no ginger in it. 'Sold at the old Welsh fairs,' says the introduction, and I wonder if then, as now, fairgoers were beguiled in the excitement of the event!

450 g (1 lb) flour
3 tsp ground ginger
3 tsp baking powder
1 tsp bicarbonate of soda
1 tsp salt
225 g (8 oz) demerara sugar

175 g (6 oz) butter
175 g (6 oz) black treacle
175 g (6 oz) golden syrup
300 ml (½ pint) milk
1 large egg, beaten

1. Grease a 23 cm (9 in) square cake tin, about 5 cm (2 in) deep, and line with buttered greaseproof paper.
2. Sift all the dry ingredients except the sugar into a bowl.
3. Warm the sugar, butter, treacle and syrup in a pan over low heat until the butter has just melted.
4. Stir the melted ingredients into the centre of the dry mixture, together with the milk and beaten egg. Beat thoroughly with a wooden spoon.
5. Pour into the prepared tin and bake in the centre of a moderate oven (gas 4, 350°F, 180°C) for 1½ hours, or until well-risen and just firm to the touch. Leave in the tin for 15 minutes, then turn out to cool on a wire rack. When cold, wrap in foil, without removing the lining paper.
6. Store for 4–7 days before cutting into chunks, to give the flavour time to mellow.

M This type of cake can be cooked in the microwave but I find the texture disappointing and don't recommend it

F Will freeze well, but hardly needs to be frozen since it keeps so well in a tin

Wholemeal sponge

Spwng blawd gwenith

With at least six working water mills in Wales it is no surprise that we can boast a fine stoneground baking tradition. Felin Geri Mill in Dyfed, an entirely water-powered 16th-century flour mill, was restored to working order from a derelict state in 1972 by Duncan Fitzwilliams and Michael Heycock. The slow and careful grinding of the grain between the stones produces flour, semolina and bran without overheating and so all the natural qualities are preserved, especially the distinctive nutty flavour which is imparted by the wheat germ oil.

175 g (6 oz) demerara sugar
150 ml (¼ pint) water
100 g (4 oz) margarine or
  butter
1 egg
2 egg yolks
175 g (6 oz) wholemeal flour
2 level tsp baking powder

1 tsp vanilla essence
150 ml (5 fl oz) double cream,
  whipped
4 tbsp rich, well-flavoured
  jam, such as damson,
  blackcurrant or plum
icing sugar to dredge

1. Grease and line two 18 cm (7 in) sandwich tins.
2. Make a sugar syrup by dissolving 50 g (2 oz) of the demerara sugar in the water, bring to the boil and allow to cool.
3. Cream the butter and the remaining sugar until light in colour and very soft in texture. Beat in the whole egg and two yolks.
4. Sieve the flour with the baking powder then gently fold into the cake mixture. Lastly add the vanilla essence with the cooled sugar water.
5. Divide the mixture between the prepared tins and bake in a moderate oven (gas 4, 350°F, 180°C) for 25–30 minutes. Leave

in the tins to cool for 15 minutes before turning out on to a
cooling rack.

6. Sandwich the two sponges together with the cream and jam.
Dust the top with icing sugar.

M   Suitable for microwave cookery

F   Freeze well wrapped, allow extra time for cream to thaw

Teisen Lap

This recipe is taken from Minwel Tibbott's book *Welsh Fare*, in which she describes how this 'moist' cake (for that is the literal translation for *lap*) served the miners well for their lunch. It didn't crumble or make them too thirsty so was the ideal 'filler' to pack into their lunch boxes and take down the pit. Originally Teisen Lap would have been cooked in a shallow tin in front of the open fire, and to get the same texture today you must grill it slowly. An equally delicious cake can be made by baking in a hot oven.

225 g (8 oz) flour
½ tsp baking powder
pinch of salt
grated nutmeg
50 g (2 oz) butter

50 g (2 oz) caster sugar
50 g (2 oz) sultanas and
   currants, mixed
1 large or 2 small eggs, beaten
a little milk to moisten

1. Sieve the flour, baking powder, salt and nutmeg. Rub in the butter, add the sugar, fruit and eggs.
2. Add the milk gradually, beating with a wooden spoon, until you have a mixture soft enough to drop, albeit reluctantly, from the spoon.
3. Bake in a greased and lined shallow tin in a moderately hot oven (gas 5, 375°F, 190°C) for about 30 minutes until golden brown and well-risen.

M   From a purist's point of view I don't recommend that Teisen Lap should be cooked in a microwave. However, who knows, perhaps contemporary miners' wives bake theirs in microwave ovens today!

F   Freeze well wrapped, whole or in slices

Stoneground wholemeal bread
Bara gwenith

'In my childhood we took oats, wheat and barley to the local mill, and after discussion with the miller, we arrived at the exact kind of fineness best suited to our taste, and the exact amount of husk to be left in the final product.' *Give Me Yesterday* by James Williams.

Nothing tempts the palate more than the smell of freshly baked bread. With the advent of easy-blend yeast which is added directly to the flour, homemade bread takes on a whole new 'easy' look. Ideally, stoneground flour produced by a traditional water mill should be used, so do collect some from one of the restored mills in Wales next time you visit.

Makes 2 large loaves

1.5 kg (3.3 lb) wholemeal flour
1 level tbsp salt
25 g (1 oz) fat or butter
2 sachets easy-blend dried yeast
1 dsp soft brown sugar
900 ml (1½ pints) warm water

1. Add salt to the flour and rub in the fat. Stir in the yeast and sugar.
2. Pour in the water and start to knead immediately. Work the dough for about 5 minutes until it is smooth and elastic.
3. Divide the dough into 2, shape and place in two 900 g (2 lb) warmed, greased loaf tins. Cover and leave to rise in a warm place for about 30 minutes or until the dough has doubled in size.
4. Bake in the middle of a moderately hot oven (gas 6, 400°F, 200°C) for 35–40 minutes. Alternatively, divide the dough

into buns and bake for about 15 minutes at the same temperature.

M   If you like microwave bread, which I do, pop it under a hot grill to give the crust a little colour as soon as it comes out of the microwave

F   All bread freezes well, this loaf included

Shell shortbread
Teisen beffro

Beffro is short for Aberffraw, in Anglesey, the seat of the Welsh Parliament. These simple little shortbread cakes were originally baked in scallop shells, which gave them an unusual shape with pretty markings. If you don't have any shells or a decorative pastry cutter then cut the shortbread into rounds and mark each with the shape of a shell. Ideal cooking for children, and just the type of 'nibble' you will be offered should you visit Llanfairpwllgwyngyllgogerychwyrndrobwllllantysiliogogogoch railway station on Anglesey!

Makes 25–30

175 g (6 oz) butter   100 g (4 oz) caster sugar, plus
225 g (8 oz) flour   extra for dredging

1. Rub the butter into the flour until the mixture resembles fine breadcrumbs. Stir in the sugar.
2. Using your fingertips press the mixture together and knead to a smooth pliable paste. Roll out fairly thinly on a well-floured board and cut into 5 cm (2 in) circles. Using the tip of a sharp-bladed knife mark each with a scallop shell pattern.
3. Bake in a moderately hot oven (gas 5, 375°F, 190°C) for about 10 minutes until the biscuits turn a pale golden colour.
4. Cool on the baking tray and when cold sprinkle lavishly with caster sugar. Store in an airtight tin for up to a week.

M   These shell shortbreads are quite successful in the micro-wave, if rather pale in appearance

F   Good biscuits to freeze

Farmhouse oatcakes
Bara ceirch ffermdy

Oatcakes are a Celtic speciality which you will still find griddled in Scotland and Ireland as well as Wales. Varying in size and shape these coarse-textured, nutty biscuits are delicious with cheese. This recipe was given to me by Lynda Kettle, one of the most inspired cooks I know. She not only runs a bustling farm guesthouse in Snowdonia, but feeds her visitors almost exclusively on home-produced foods, including her own farmhouse cheese, preserves, breads and vegetables.

To save time I suggest that you bake these oatcakes by the trayful in the oven, although a heavy frying pan or griddle would produce an authentic oatcake for the purist.

Makes 15

100 g (4 oz) wholemeal flour
35 g (1½ oz) medium oatmeal
3 tsp soft brown sugar
½ tsp salt
1 tsp baking powder

½ tsp cayenne pepper
75 g (3 oz) salted Welsh butter
   or bacon fat
Milk to bind if necessary

1. Mix all the dry ingredients making sure the cayenne pepper is evenly distributed throughout.
2. Melt the butter or bacon fat and stir into the dry ingredients. Add enough milk to make a fairly stiff dough.
3. On a board dusted with wholemeal flour roll the dough out fairly thinly, about 0.25 cm (⅛ in) thick, and using a 6 cm (2½ in) biscuit cutter stamp into circles.
4. Bake on a baking sheet in a warm oven (gas 3, 325°F, 170°C) for about 20–30 minutes until pale golden.

M   Try them in the microwave; they won't be the same as when baked in the conventional oven but you may prefer them

F   Ideal for freezing, well wrapped

Llanddarog Fair cakes
Teisennau Ffair Llanddarog

Do try these tempting little cakes, for their richness and simplicity make them a favourite with both cook and consumer. Originally made for Llanddarog Fair in Carmarthenshire they must have held a place of affection at the turn of the century as the toffee apple does today. Traditionally these cakes were baked in a Dutch oven – a covered tray which would sit on the hearth beside the glowing embers and cook by indirect heat.

225 g (8 oz) butter
350 g (12 oz) self-raising flour
175 g (6oz) caster sugar, plus
  extra for dredging

3 tbsp beer
100 g (4oz) currants

1. Rub the butter into the flour then add the sugar and currants.
2. Mix in the beer to form a soft dough and roll out on a floured board to about 1 cm (½ in) thick.
3. Cut into 5 cm (2 in) rounds with a pastry cutter and bake in a moderate oven (gas 4, 350°F, 180°C) for 15 minutes. Dust with caster sugar.

M   As with most baking which incorporates self-raising flour, the texture of these little cakes will change with microwave cooking. Do try, and see if you like them; perhaps bake some in the oven and some in the microwave

F   Very suitable for freezing

Honey and ginger cake

Teisen mel a sinsir

I have taken this recipe from Minwel Tibbott's *Welsh Fare*. It comes from Llanwenog in Cardiganshire and it is interesting to see that honey is the only form of sweetening used. The cook who originally gave the recipe to Minwel Tibbott used cup measurements, which have been repeated here, and I suggest that you use a large teacup for all measures and follow the recipe as for gingerbread by adding all the liquid at once. It has a flavour that improves with keeping and should be left for two weeks before cutting.

4 cups flour
2 heaped tsp baking powder
pinch of salt
2 heaped tsp ground ginger
½ cup sultanas
a little candied peel, chopped

½ cup cherries, halved
100 g (4 oz) butter
¾ cup honey
a little milk
2 eggs, beaten

1. Sift the flour, baking powder, salt and ginger into a bowl and add the sultanas, candied peel and cherries.
2. Melt the butter over a low heat and dissolve the honey in it with a little milk. Leave to cool, then pour, together with the beaten eggs, into the dry mixture. Stir thoroughly.
3. Bake in a greased cake tin in a moderately hot oven (gas 5, 375°F, 190°C) for 45–60 minutes.
4. Store the cake for a fortnight before cutting . . . if you can!

M   Not suitable for microwave cooking

F   No need to freeze when it keeps so well in an airtight tin

Caerphilly scones
Sgonau Caerffili

This recipe suits today's taste for wholemeal savoury food. The combination of stoneground wholemeal flour and tasty Caerphilly cheese is a winner and a little sugar added to the dough brings out the taste of the cheese. In fact a pocketful of Caerphilly scones would be really comforting during a trip down one of the coal mines or slate quarries. More and more of these mines are opening to the public and they give the tourist a fascinating glimpse of how Wales's mineral wealth has been won. Well worth a visit.

Makes 8

225 g (8 oz) wholemeal self-raising flour
salt and cayenne pepper
35 g (1½ oz) butter

50 g (2 oz) Caerphilly cheese, grated
12 g (½ oz) caster sugar
150 ml (¼ pint) milk, plus milk to glaze

1. Mix the seasoning into the flour then rub in the butter. Add the cheese and sugar and enough milk to make a soft but firm dough.
2. Turn on to a floured board, knead as quickly and lightly as possible and pat the dough out to about 4 cm (1½ in) deep – this is quicker than using a rolling pin.
3. Shape into scones with a knife or pastry cutter and place on a greased baking sheet. Brush with milk and bake in a hot oven (gas 7, 425°F, 220°C) for 10 minutes. Serve hot from the oven, well buttered.

M   These scones will microwave well

F   Freeze well wrapped. They will thaw in minutes so don't remove from the freezer before needed. Alternatively, reheat from frozen

Buttermilk bread

Bara llaeth enwyn

Buttermilk, once an integral part of Welsh country life, is rarely sold now direct from the farm. As an ingredient in baking it was essential, as a remedy for gastric illnesses it was unbeatable, and as a refreshing drink there was none better. Today it is possible to buy cultured buttermilk which has been pasteurized and the lactic acid reintroduced. It is these lactic acid-producing enzymes that give buttermilk its special qualities, and when mixed with baking powder in breads or cakes a magical lightness appears.

450 g (1 lb) flour
1 tsp baking powder
25 g (1 oz) butter
25 g (1 oz) caster sugar

100 g (4 oz) mixed dried fruit
300 ml (½ pint) buttermilk
beaten egg or milk to glaze

1. In a large bowl combine the flour and baking powder and rub in the butter. Stir in the sugar and dried fruit.
2. Pour in the buttermilk and stir briskly until you have a soft dough. Turn immediately on to a floured board and knead into shape – oblong for a 900 g (2 lb) loaf tin or into two rounds if you prefer. Score the dough across with the tip of a sharp knife.
3. Glaze with beaten egg or milk and bake in a moderately hot oven (gas 6, 400°F, 200°C) until firm – approximately 45 minutes for a tin loaf, 30 minutes for rounds. Leave to cool, and serve sliced and buttered.

M   Cook in the microwave, but pop under a hot grill to brown before serving

F   All breads freeze well. Wrap in foil or polythene

Crunchy bran fingers
Bisgedi bran

This is a recipe from the Felin Crewi water mill at Penegoes near Machynlleth in Powys. Having seen round the mill, visitors fill the café and these delicious fingers vanish as fast as they appear on the counter.

Makes 24

225 g (8 oz) butter or margarine
100 g (4 oz) soft brown sugar
25 g (1 oz) bran

300 g (11 oz) 100% wholewheat flour
½ tsp cinnamon

1. Cream the butter and sugar until very soft and light in colour. Fold in the bran, flour and cinnamon, and mix well.
2. Tip the mixture into a well-greased 25 cm × 20 cm (10 in × 8 in) Swiss roll tin and level with a palette knife so that it is about 0.5 cm (¼ in) thick. Press all round the edges with your fingers. Mark into 24 fingers with a knife and prick all over with a fork.
3. Bake in a moderately hot oven (gas 5, 375°F, 190°C) for about 30 minutes until golden brown. Leave in the tin to cool for about 5 minutes, then carefully lift the biscuits on to a cooling tray.

● Serve on their own or with a soft pudding such as a fool.

M   Try! The taste and texture will be altered but it might be to your liking

F   Suitable for freezing

Apple cake
Teisen afal

This recipe was given to me by Eluned Lloyd who often bakes it at her guest house in Newport, Pembrokeshire. 'It is a very popular Welsh dish which disappears quickly in our restaurant,' she says, and if you try it you'll know why!

Just to show what a variety of words the Welsh language offers, let me say that this recipe for apple cake translates to *cacen afal* in North Wales, *teisen* and *cacen* both meaning 'cake'.

125 g (4 oz) butter or
  margarine
125 g (4 oz) soft brown sugar
2 eggs
rind and juice of 1 lemon
225 g (8 oz) wholemeal self-
  raising flour

1 tsp cinnamon
4 eating apples, peeled, cored
  and sliced
honey or golden syrup to
  serve

1. Butter a 20 cm (8 in) square tin or a 450 g (1 lb) loaf tin.
2. Cream together the butter and sugar, beating hard, and always for longer than you anticipate. Add the eggs with the lemon juice and rind.
3. Fold in the flour and cinnamon, which will give a fairly stiff consistency, and put the mixture in the tin.
4. Arrange the apple slices all over the top of the sponge mixture so that they stick up rather like bristles on a hedgehog. Flick a little water over the top.
5. Bake in a moderately hot oven (gas 5, 375°F, 190°C) for 40–50 minutes or until a sharp knife inserted into the centre of the cake comes out clean. Dribble honey or golden syrup over the top and serve hot or cold.

M   Cook in the microwave and glaze under the grill to brown the apple slices

F   Freezes well, whole or sliced

DRINKS AND PRESERVES

Iced honey fruit tea
Mead
Mulled wine
Boozy fruit
Chutney in the raw
Pear chutney
Apple and mint chutney
Redcurrant and apple sauce
Rhubarb and gooseberry jam
Plum and ginger jam

Who knows how long and hard next winter will be? Imagine living on a windswept mountain in one of the remote parts of Wales: half a mile from your nearest neighbour and with no chance of contact with the outside world once the snow arrives. Self-sufficiency strikes a keen note, for there will be no groceries delivered; how those jars of jam and preserves stored away in the larder will be appreciated then.

During the long summer days and those warm and blustery autumn weekends, there is always time to gather a little fruit and preserve it, safe in the knowledge that no artificial preservatives have been incorporated, no extra sugar added to help it to set. Make your own jams and enjoy a feeling of self-sufficiency as experienced by so many rural families in Wales. What could make a better present for a special friend than a jar of something that you have made yourself? Homemade jam, chutneys and pickles, bottles of homemade cordials or fruits steeped in alcohol – all these will appear as jewels on the pantry shelf to brighten the dullest of February days. So make the most of the fruit crops as they come into season, collect your produce when the quality is at a premium but the price at its lowest and preserve and store it away for gloomy winter days ahead.

Iced honey fruit tea

Te claear gyda mel a ffrwyth

Iced tea is a favourite with Americans, and as a refreshing drink it is hard to beat. Try this honeyed tea and perhaps you too will be converted away from that steaming hot 'cuppa'.

Makes about 12 cup servings

1.2 l (2 pints) water
1½ tsp tea (Indian or China)
5 whole cloves
300 ml (½ pint) orange juice
1.2 l (2 pints) lime juice (or made-up cordial)

juice of 2 lemons
4 tbsp honey

To garnish
thin orange slices
fresh red cherries
mint leaves

1. Boil the water and pour over tea and cloves. Cover and leave to infuse for 5 minutes then strain.
2. Combine tea with remaining ingredients and pour over cracked ice to chill.
3. Serve in a large jug garnished with the orange slices, cherries and mint leaves.

Mead
Medd

Mead was much praised by the Welsh poets and bards who promoted the qualities of this 'royal' beverage.

Makes approx 15 × 75 cl
  bottles

50 g (2 oz) fresh yeast
small piece of bread
9 l (2 gallons) water
2.25 l (4 pints) honey

900 g (2 lb) white sugar
juice of 4 lemons
25 g (1 oz) cloves
piece of root ginger, grated

1. Spread the yeast on the bread.
2. Boil the water, adding the honey and sugar, and pour into an earthenware pot. Skim off any scum.
3. Add lemon juice, cloves and ginger and leave to cool.
4. When just warm float the bread and yeast on top. Cover with a clean cloth and leave to stand for 6–8 days.
5. Strain and bottle the mead, leaving the corks loose. It will be ready to drink after 5–6 months.

Mulled wine

Gwin cynhesol

This ever-popular drink which warms both body and soul in deep winter, was a favourite throughout the Middle Ages. The ancient Celts might have called it *piment*, the Germans refer to it as *Glühwein* but I like to call it mulled or even spiced wine.

Serves 6–8

bottle of red wine – the quality really isn't important
½ wine bottleful water
2 tbsp brandy

1 tsp ground ginger, or a 1 cm (½ in) cube of fresh root ginger
1 tsp ground cinnamon
1 tbsp honey
1 orange, cut in half
½ lemon, cut in half

1. Put all the ingredients into a large saucepan and heat gently, stirring well. Don't let the mixture boil but let it 'stew' for a while to allow the fruit and spices to blend into the wine.
2. Serve, not too hot, in mugs or glasses, with a napkin since it tends to become very sticky.

M   Once made, mulled wine reheats well by the mug in the microwave

Boozy fruit

Ffrwythau mewn gwirod

What better way to preserve summer and autumn fruits than to store them in alcohol? After just a couple of weeks the fruit tastes delicious, but the longer you leave it in the alcohol the better the juices taste.

The timing is perfect too, for if you collect summer soft fruits or autumn berries and immerse them in your choice of spirit then tuck them away out of sight for a couple of months they can reappear to become the star attraction for Christmas celebrations. Make a little extra and you have the ideal Christmas present for friends!

Imagine a bleak winter's evening with foul weather outside and too many bills to pay; how delightfully decadent to ease the misery with a sip of plum-flavoured gin, or brandy that has been mixed with fresh, sun-ripened apricots for the past four months. If the syrup is good to sip, then imagine how a spoonful of boozy fruit will liven up a pudding or a bowl of ice cream!

First you must choose your fruit. Any of the summer berries – strawberries, raspberries, or the currant family – will do, and in late summer and autumn you can choose from juicy plums, apricots, blackberries and, of course, sloes. Then select the alcohol you prefer. Gin is traditional for sloes, but plums and damsons also flavour gin well, and are much less effort, since the gathering and preparing of sloes is almost a labour of love. Vodka is a good spirit to use since it has little flavour, no colour, but lots of alcohol! Or make a German *Rumtopf* – this mixture of summer fruits soaked in rum is very special, and can also work well using brandy.

The fruit must be in perfect condition. Pick it over very

carefully and discard any cut, bruised, underripe or overripe fruits. Then layer it up with half its weight of sugar (caster or granulated will do) and leave overnight. Next day tip the fruit and sugar into clean jars with secure tops. Jam jars, kilner jars or pottery jars are all suitable but I find that jars with narrow necks are best. The reason for this is that it is important to immerse all the fruit in the liquid with none popping above the surface, and with a wide-necked jar it can be a problem to keep the fruit down. However, one answer to this problem is to cut a plastic disc from an old ice-cream container and then fit this into the top of the jar, thus forcing the fruit down into the liquid. If the fruit makes contact with the air it will possibly go mouldy and ruin the whole jar – which would be a tragedy!

Allow 600 ml (1 pint) of alcohol to every 450 g (1 lb) prepared fruit, and just pour it over the fruit in the jar, fix the plastic disc on top of the fruit and secure the jar with its lid. Keep in a cool, dark place and give the jar a slight shake or a couple of turns every day for a couple of weeks until the sugar has dissolved. Keep the boozy fruit for at least two months, longer if you possibly can; it will be worth waiting for.

Chutney in the raw
Catwad amrwd

This is the very simplest of chutneys to prepare. The end result is rather like piccalilli; crunchy, spicy and very moreish. Make up a whole saucepanful in the autumn when there are plenty of marrows about and it will be mellow and delicious in time for the cold turkey at Christmas.

Makes approx. 8 × 450 g (1 lb) jars

1 medium marrow
1 cauliflower
1 cucumber
3 carrots
3 large onions
275 g (10 oz) salt
2.8 l (5 pints) water

For the sauce
75 g (3 oz) flour
1 tsp curry powder
1 tbsp mustard powder
1 tsp turmeric
550 g (1¼ lb) granulated
  sugar
600 ml (1 pint) malt or
  pickling vinegar

1. Peel, deseed and chop the marrow. Divide the cauliflower into sprigs.
2. Dice the cucumber, unskinned. Grate or finely chop the carrots and onions.
3. Put all the prepared vegetables in a large bowl, sprinkle the salt over the top, pour in the water and leave overnight.
4. For the sauce; in a large saucepan blend all the dry ingredients with a little vinegar to make a smooth paste then add the rest of the vinegar.
5. Heat gently until boiling, stir well and cook until thick. This will take about 5 minutes.
6. Drain the vegetables well, pressing out the liquid, then toss them into the sauce. Cook through for a further 5 minutes.

7. Leave the pickle to cool completely then spoon into clean, dry jars and seal with jam-pot covers. Store for at least a month before eating.

Pear chutney

Catwad gellyg

A good way to use up those pear windfalls. Use either ripe or hard pears to make this tangy chutney, and cut away any bruising and blemishes.

Makes approx. 5 × 450 g (1 lb) jars

450 g (1 lb) onions, peeled and chopped or grated
600 ml (1 pint) malt vinegar
900 g (2 lb) pears, peeled, cored and chopped
100 g (4 oz) dates, chopped
2 tsp pickling spice
1 tbsp salt

1 dsp ground ginger or 2.5 cm (1 in) cube fresh root ginger, grated.
3 cloves garlic, crushed (optional)
1 tsp cayenne pepper
675 g (1½ lb) granulated sugar

1. Put the onion in a large preserving pan, add 150 ml (¼ pint) vinegar and stew gently for 10 minutes until the onion is soft.
2. Add the chopped pears, dates, pickling spice (tied securely in a muslin bag), salt, ginger, garlic and cayenne and just enough vinegar to stop the mixture from burning.
3. Cook gently until the fruit is soft, stirring from time to time. Add the remaining vinegar and all the sugar, stirring very well, and boil steadily until the chutney is thick.
4. Remove pickling spices, pour the chutney into warm, clean, dry jars and seal. Leave for at least a month, longer if possible, before serving. This gives it a chance to mellow and for the flavours to blend.

Apple and mint chutney
Catwad afal a mintys

This is the perfect partner for cold Welsh lamb. The sweet, minty flavour of this chutney also tastes good with cold poultry, tongue or sausages.

Follow the recipe for pear chutney, omitting the ginger and cayenne pepper and substituting apples for pears. Add 1½ tbsp chopped mint to the mixture just before bottling.

Redcurrant and apple sauce

Saws afal a chwrens coch

Delicious with roast meat, poultry or game, hot or cold.

Makes 450 g (1 lb)

225 g (8 oz) ripe redcurrants
150 ml (¼ pint) water
225 g (8 oz) apples, peeled,
  cored and chopped weight

3–4 tbsp granulated sugar
knob of butter
6 cardamom pods, seeds
  removed and ground

1. Put the redcurrants in a saucepan with half the water and simmer gently until soft. Sieve the pulp.
2. Combine the chopped apples, remaining water, redcurrant purée, sugar, butter and ground cardamom, and simmer until the apples are soft.
3. Beat the mixture hard with a wooden spoon until smooth and shiny.
4. Pack into small containers and keep in the fridge for 2–3 weeks.

M   Suitable for microwave cookery

F   Suitable for freezing

Jams

To my mind the most vital piece of equipment when it comes to jam making is a sugar thermometer. You can take all the care in the world with the preparation of the fruit, and follow all the instructions to make a perfect jam, but it just won't set until it reaches the right temperature. With a thermometer clipped to the side of your saucepan, you can tell at a glance when to start testing the jam to see if it's set, and so avoid wastage by overboiling – and save your temper by not testing too soon and too often.

Rhubarb and gooseberry jam

Jam riwbob ac eirin mair

This is a lovely jam, with a fragrant flavour. The recipe comes from *Good Cookery*, written by Lady Llanover in 1867.

'Boil an equal quantity of rhubarb cut up, and gooseberries before they are quite ripe, with ¾ of a pound of crystalized moist sugar to one pound of fruit. When boiled, it will make excellent jam, similar to apricot.'

Let me interpret:

900 g (2 lb) rhubarb, cut into 2.5 cm (1 in) lengths
900 g (2 lb) unripe or firm gooseberries, topped and tailed

1.35 k (3 lb) granulated sugar
juice of 1 lemon

1. Put the rhubarb and gooseberries in a large preserving pan with the sugar and lemon juice. Leave to steep for a couple of hours.
2. Bring to the boil slowly, over gentle heat, stirring all the time until the sugar has dissolved.
3. Boil rapidly until the jam sets lightly or forms a skin when a spoonful is placed on a saucer.
4. Take off the heat and let the jam cool slightly before pouring into warm, clean, dry jam jars. Seal as instructed on packet of jam-pot covers.

Plum and ginger jam

Jam eirin a sinsir

Makes 2 × 450 g (1 lb) jars

450 g (1 lb) firm plums   1 tsp ground ginger
450 g (1 lb) granulated sugar   75 ml (3 fl oz) water

1. Stone the plums, crack the plum stones and reserve the kernels.
2. In a large preserving pan stew the plums gently over low heat until they begin to break up. Add the water only if the juices don't appear fairly quickly. Once the fruit begins to collapse, turn up the heat and simmer until the plums are completely soft and pulpy.
3. Add the sugar and ginger and stir until dissolved, then boil rapidly until setting point is reached.
4. Cool slightly, then stir well to distribute the fruit evenly and pour into warmed, clean, dry jam jars. Seal as instructed on packet of jam-pot covers.

WILD WALES

'Mother made wine from cowslips, parsnips, elderberry, elderflower, damson and gorse flower. The gorse petals were picked
when the sun beat fiercely upon them and taken hurriedly
home and put into a vat. The gorseflower wine left no hangover
but the effect of a few glasses was to make one feel Olympian,
one of the Gods.' *Give Me Yesterday* by James Williams.

Wild Wales is ripe for the picking. With almost 1600 square
miles of National Park, land almost untouched by commercial
agriculture or industry, there is a superb lack of cultivation in
many areas. Look at Snowdonia in the north, surrounded by
wild and beautiful land, travel down to the unspoilt area full of
natural resources in mid Wales, make your way to the Brecon
Beacons or, away to the far south west, the Pembrokeshire
Coast National Park. Wander down the Wye valley, over the
Black Mountains, traverse the Taf, Teifi and Towy rivers of
South Wales, or meander over the heathers of North Wales,
beside the lakes of Bala and Padarn or down by the River
Conwy.

Tender shoots of marsh samphire taste delicious, crisp and
salty just as they are. Pick them in the summer from July to
September off the sand or mud flats around the coast of
Pembrokeshire. Watch the indigenous Welsh collecting laver off
the rocks along the Gower and Pembrokeshire coast and prepare some for a tasty breakfast (see p. 50) Arm yourself with a
'scraper' and go to it scratching cockles out of the sand, or fill
some buckets full of mussels for a meal of distinction. All you
need is a little time, patience and perhaps the company of a
Welshman who is willing to tell a few tales of his youth. And
so time flies and your bucket is full.

Jam making, pickling fruit or turning it into chutney are some of the more rewarding jobs in the kitchen. Gather your fruit and a few friends and helpers, and prepare a larder full of jars to last through the long winter months when we really need a taste of summer.

The Welsh have been using herbs in medicine longer than any other region of the British Isles. As far back as 1,000 B.C. the priests and teachers, or *gwyddoniaid* as they were known, used a variety of wild herbs to cure the sick. Later, during the 13th century, a collection of medical recipes was compiled by the physicians of Myddfai. These physicians, according to legend and folklore, originally obtained their healing skills centuries earlier through magic. There is a fabulous story behind this; look out for it as the legend of the Lady of the Lake.

At this time apothecaries would send out herb gatherers to collect healing herbs from the countryside, and with the current fashion in herbalism there has been a revival in the cultivation of these herbs. A few herbs which have always been synonymous with the Welsh are savory fach, a vital ingredient in faggots, wild thyme, marjoram, tansy, and rosemary used in powder form to flavour cakes. Ginger, brought back along with so many exotic spices by the Crusaders, found a place in the hearts of the Welsh, and it has added a much needed zip to many basic dishes.

Flowers such as elderberry, clover, marigold, nasturtium and violets have been incorporated in Welsh cooking for some time, adding flavour and colour to sweet and savoury dishes alike. See the recipe for Granny Griffiths' cawl (p. 56) for a novel way to use marigold petals!

Country wines were just as much a part of rural Welsh life as were fruit pies and tarts. Most households made a variety of wines from the hedgerows – fragrant elderberry or gooseberry, blackberry or blackcurrant – and this rewarding hobby is still much practised today. Ready in as little as six weeks, these sometimes potent wines were used medicinally as a pick-me-up, or sometimes served, like Madeira, with a cake at teatime.

Viniculture is practised in a small way throughout South Wales. Alas, the commercial viability of these small vineyards is threatened more by the addition of duty than by our inclement weather, and most vines are grown as a hobby rather than a business. A selection of grapes is used from both German and French vines, resulting in a good flavour from hardy plants. Müller-Thurgau, Seyval Blanc and Madeleine-Angevine are the most favoured grapes, and combined they produce a light, dry and very palatable wine. None of the vineyards is of sufficient size to process its own grapes so the milling, pressing and fermenting take place in England.

Bees, honey and mead come to mind when we think of Welsh food. Honey was, of course, used as one of the earliest sweeteners before those dreaded white sugar granules arrived to ruin our teeth, and it has always been taken by the health-conscious. Welsh lamb benefits greatly from a coating of honey, and Welsh honey will never be out of favour with the tourist, even though it is sold at a premium. Visit the Royal Welsh Agricultural Show at Builth Wells and you will be astounded by the large number of exhibitors showing beeswax candles, honeycombs and mead.

Talking of mead, the defeat and slaughter of the Welsh at the Battle of Catraeth has been attributed, alas, to the mead they drank to excess beforehand.

Beer and cider have been brewed in Welsh homes in the past but no longer, for we have fine breweries which produce famous beer which is consumed in enormous quantities, especially in conjunction with the national game of rugby football.

Enough, let's get back to the wild side of Wales. Take your basket and head for the hedgerows, coastal paths, damp woodlands and dry heathlands. Find a host of berries, mushrooms, seaweeds, shellfish, wild flowers and herbs. Don't hurry but enjoy collecting your free food and use it as did our ancestors over the centuries.

WELSH CHEESES

There is something in the gentle acidity of a good farm Caerphilly, says cheesemaker Gill Bond, that relates very closely to the soil, the water and the gentle light that falls in the deeper valleys of Wales. Over the past fifteen years Gill has researched traditional cheesemaking in Wales and now produces a Caerphilly that her elderly farming neighbours assure her tastes just as Caerphilly used to!

The Welsh have always loved cheese. 'Brined cheese' such as Caerphilly was part of the settlement made between feuding members of a family under the Laws of Hywel Dda, a Welsh prince who instigated the first legal system in the 10th century, bringing together many ancient customs and rules.

Professor Rhys, of the Royal Commission on Land in Wales and Monmouthshire in 1895, has this to say about Caerphilly: 'The colliers have found that it is not a crumbly cheese, and that is why it is so useful in Wales, you see if they go down into the pit and take it with them it does not crumble and they are able to eat it.' The shape and size of traditional Caerphilly, 4 cm (1½ in) thick and 38 cm (15 in) broad, also made a good-sized wedge to eat down the pit, and the miners were willing to pay more than twice the price for it than, say, a semi-skimmed-milk cheese.

During the last century cheeses made from skimmed milk were, however, in the majority. Poverty in rural Wales taught strict discipline and self-sufficiency to the farmers. First, they took the fat from the milk to make butter which, being well salted, would keep during the cold winter months, and the remaining skimmed milk was turned into a semi-hard, lightly pressed, often rather unpleasant-tasting cheese with a none-too-good texture. However, this cheese could be made very palatable by slicing it thickly and roasting it in front of the open fire – Welsh Rarebit, as we now know it. The cheese could be sold at the market 10–21 days after making for as little as 3p per lb and was eaten fresh, as was Caerphilly, which would reach 7p per lb. Ewe's milk was sometimes added to the skimmed cow's milk and this resulted in an altogether better and richer cheese. In *Good Cookery* (1867) Lady Llanover says 'the proportion for cheese was one quart of ewe's milk to thirty quarts of cow's milk'.

Goat's milk was traditionally used for cheesemaking until the 18th century. With a yield of more than 2 quarts a day the Welsh goat could provide a nourishing, wholesome cheese which had a fine flavour and creamy texture much superior to that made from skimmed cow's milk.

Alas, many basic cheesemaking skills were lost during the First World War. Times were hard and many dairy farmers were only rescued by the advent of the Milk Marketing Board in 1933, which bought their milk and guaranteed a regular income. But if throughout the British Isles the traditional cheesemaking crafts were neglected earlier this century, then they are now enjoying a healthy revival, and nowhere more prolifically than in Wales.

With the application of modern hygiene and science to traditional recipes we can now boast a superb range of quality farmhouse cheeses made by more than thirty producers throughout the principality. By helping each other, these new cheesemakers are spreading their skills through the rural communities, and the variety of cheese available in Wales is astounding – hard pressed Cheddars, ewe's-milk cheese, moorland goat's cheese, soft cheese in profusion, and of course, Caerphilly is back on the map again.

To the customer the benefits are paramount. We can now choose between a factory-made cheese with uniform texture and taste, or the mature flavour of a farmhouse cheese with a character of its own, which may differ from cheese to cheese. Of course, the difference lies in the milk, and the majority of Welsh cheeses are made with unpasteurized milk from organically reared cows. It is this that adds the character to our farmhouse cheeses.

Pasteurization is the process of heating milk to 71.7°C for 15 seconds, thereby killing all harmful bacteria. A necessary precaution, you may say, but it also kills off the bacteria which encourage milk to ripen naturally, which in turn leads to the natural maturing of the cheese. So cheeses made with unpasteurized milk nearly always have a fuller flavour, although the stability cannot be guaranteed and some will ripen more quickly than others.

The flavour of the milk must also be affected by the well-being of the cows themselves. A healthy cow eating midsummer grass grown on fertile soil on a warm, sunny day will produce milk of a quality which is second to none. And dairy farmers in Wales are aware that antibiotics such as penicillin tend to interfere with the cheesemaking process, as do pesticides, the residues of which became concentrated in the soil and thus in the grass on which the cows feed.

Start with contented cows and take their milk. Evening milk is richer than morning milk, so often a combination of the two is used. This milk is allowed to stand in a vat overnight to ripen naturally before a starter of lactic acid bacteria is added, which speeds up the souring process. The bacteria converts the milk sugar into lactic acid and helps the milk to coagulate. Once the milk has soured, rennet is added and this is stimulated by the calcium in the milk to convert the protein, known as casein, into a junket-like mass called curd.

The next stage is to cut the curd in order to let the whey drain out. This must be done very slowly and carefully, especially at the beginning, to prevent the fat escaping from the curd. Horizontal and vertical curd knives are used, and the separation of the whey from the curd is noticeable at once. As soon as the curd has been cut up it is stirred, usually by hand with a curd rake, to release the moisture, and at the same time it is cooked by heating the water in the jacket of the cheese vat.

When all the whey has been drained out the curd is allowed to settle at the bottom of the vat where it is cut into blocks. These are piled on top of each other and turned every ten minutes to produce a dry acid curd which is ready for milling after about fifty minutes. Once the curd has been milled into small granules salt is added and mixed in thoroughly, and

finally the curd is packed into cheesecloth-lined moulds ready
for pressing. It is pressed gently at first, with more pressure
being applied each day until it is eventually transformed into a
closely knit cheese.

The cheese is left to ripen and it loses some moisture, thus
becoming more solid and containing a higher proportion of dry
matter. At this stage it begins to acquire the familiar taste of
cheese. Complicated chemical processes are taking place as the
protein decomposes, and acids and other elements are released
through the cheese, influencing its taste and aroma. Ammonia
may be formed and its pungent odour can be detected in the
cheese-ripening room. The cheese is then matured for six weeks
to twelve months, depending on the flavour and texture
required.

Today in Wales, as in the past, the regional variations provide
a wonderful range of textures and flavours, many of which are
now available throughout Britain. Look out for the following
Welsh cheeses in specialist cheese shops and some supermarkets nationwide.

ACORN. Made in Bethania, near Llanon in Dyfed. A ewe's-
milk cheese, full fat, hard pressed, with vegetarian rennet. The
milk is home-produced and completely free from herbicides,
pesticides and chemical fertilizers. Acorn may be suitable for
those allergic to cow's or goat's milk.

CARDIGAN. Made in Lampeter from organic cow's milk with
vegetarian rennet. In texture a cross between Cheddar and
Caerphilly, mild in flavour when young but matures well.
Available all the year round in discs of 3.4–3.6 k (7½–8 lb).

CAWS CENARTH. Traditional Caerphilly and Cheddar made
from the farm herd of pedigree Friesian and Holstein dairy
cattle. The cheeses are sold in presentation boxes of 400 g
(14 oz) minis, or 900 g (2 lb) and 4 k (9 lb) wheels.

NEVERN DAIRIES. Traditional Cheddar made with home-
produced milk from pedigree Friesian cows. Bandaged, rinded
and larded Cheddar, and Red Cheddar. Pasteurized and unpasteurized cheeses and vegetarian Cheddar with non-animal

rennet and palm oil to seal the rind. Open textured, mild, mature and very mature cheeses available.

PANT-Y-GAWN FARM GOAT'S CHEESE. A soft, white, creamy cheese made from pasteurized goat's milk using vegetarian rennet. Mild, non-goaty flavour, easily spread. Available plain, herb, coated with black pepper, green and red sweet pepper, and even sweet with black cherry and brandy or honey and spices.

PLAS DAIRY FARM CHEESE. Low-fat, spreadable, cow's and goat's cheese made in Anglesey from lactic curd. Natural and garlic-and-herb flavours.

SKIRRID EWE'S-MILK CHEESE. Made in Gwent from a farm which overlooks the Skirrid Mountain. Using unpasteurized sheep's milk, pure sea salt and vegetarian rennet the cheeses are marinated in mead before being matured for three months prior to being sold. A firm, white cheese with a natural rind and mild flavour.

TEIFI. A Gouda-type cheese made in Llandyssul, Dyfed. Semi-hard with a creamy texture. Low fat, made from unpasteurized, partly skimmed milk. Low-sodium salt used. Available plain or flavoured with chives, cumin seed, garlic, celery-and-garlic, garlic-and-onion, mustard seed or sweet pepper.

These Welsh cheeses and others may well find their way on to the dinner table anywhere from Dundee down to Dover. You may find them neatly packaged in supermarket chilled cabinets and they will at least offer you a sample of the range of cheeses made in Wales.

But to my mind Welsh cheese is best eaten in Wales, bought from the farm, where often the visitor is encouraged to watch the cheesemaking process in action. The history of cheese and the traditional methods of cheesemaking are willingly imparted by the makers, and this is an experience that no traveller to Wales should miss.

Here are some Welsh farmhouse cheeses you should look out for in Wales:

ABERNANT. Carmarthen, Dyfed. Made from part-cow's, part-goat's milk.

BLAENWAUN MOORLAND. Whitland, Dyfed. Hard pressed goat's cheese and Caerphilly.

CAERPHILLY. Made traditionally and sold at the Castle Inn, just beside the Castle in Caerphilly, Gwent.

CALDEY ISLAND. Tenby, Dyfed. Soft lactic cheese made by the monks.

CARON GOATSMILK. Tregaron, Dyfed. Sometimes known as Harlech, a hard pressed goat's cheese.

LLANBOIDY. Login, Whitland, Dyfed. An old-style hard, full-fat cheese from milk of the rare Red Poll cattle. Available in natural mature flavour or with laverbread.

LLANGLOFFAN. Castle Morris, Dyfed. A hard, full-fat, naturally rinded cheese made with unpasteurized milk from a Jersey herd of cows.

MAESLLYN. Llandyssul, Dyfed. A traditional farmhouse Caerphilly and mature Cheddar.

MAES MAWR. Llanllyfni, Caernarfon. A hard pressed goat's cheese with natural crust.

MERLIN. Ystrad Meurig, Dyfed. Hard goat's cheese, plain or flavoured with olives.

PANTLLYN. Carmarthen, Dyfed. Farmhouse Cheddar.

PAUPER'S CHEESE. Waunfawr, Gwynedd. A soft goat's cheese with garlic and sweet herbs.

PENCARREG. Lampeter, Dyfed. A full-fat soft cow's cheese, similar to Brie.

PEN Y BONT. Carmarthen, Dyfed. A hard goat's cheese.

TYN GRUG. Lampeter, Dyfed. Mature farmhouse Cheddar.

WAUGRON. Whitland, Dyfed. A Colby-type cheese.

INDEX

Aberaeron mackerel, 99
Abergavenny chicken, 131
Ancient culinary customs, 13
Anglesey
  cake, 279
  eggs, 44
Apple(s)
  and cheese potato cake, 203
  and ginger fool, 26
  and lemon yogurt as marinade for herrings,
    62
  and mint chutney, 318
  and redcurrant sauce, 319
  cake, 304
  pancakes, 265
  pudding, Welsh, 261
  stuffing with goose, 143
  with pheasant, 121
Avocado and smoked salmon filling, with a
    roulade of fresh salmon, 105

Bacon
  and cockle pie, 74
  and leek pudding, 162
  with laverbread cakes, 50
Bain-Marie, to cook in a, 21
Bakestone (griddle), 10, 239–40, 276
  cakes, 12
Baking, 15
Bara Brith, 283
Bard's fish dish, 93
Beef, 154
  and ham loaf, 190
  in Welsh beer, 164
  mushroom and herb pie, 160
Beer, 355
  beef in Welsh, 164
Berries
  and fruit, 11
  summer, with elderflower cream, 241
  wild, 14
Biscuits, 276, 295, 296, 303
Blackberry(ies)
  and apple tart, 239
  crisp, 259
  sauce with chicken kebabs, 133
Blackcurrant layer pudding, 258
Blood pudding, 154
Boozy fruit, 313
Borrow, George, 153
Bouillabaisse, Welsh, 42
Bran fingers, crunchy, 303
Brawn, 154
Bread(s), 275–7
  and butter pudding, Welsh, 272
  buttermilk, 302
  stoneground wholemeal, 293
Broad beans in sour cream, 220

Broth
  harvest, 12
  mussel, 36
  parsley, 30
Brown bread and spinach stuffing for fillets of
    lamb, 173
Buns, honey, 286
Butter, kneaded, 20
Buttermilk, 10
  bread, 302

Caerphilly
  and mushroom pancake, 218
  cheese, 11, 326, 327, 331
  scones, 300
Cakes (sweet and savoury)
  Anglesey, 279
  apple, 304
  carrot, 278
  harvest, 12
  honey and ginger, 299
  Llanddarog Fair, 12, 298
  onion, 221
  shearing, 12
  threshing, 12
  tinker's 281
  Welsh, 280
Carrot
  and leek medley, 201
  cake, 278
Cawl, 10, 13
  Ceredigion, 60
  Granny Griffiths', 56, 324
  Michaelmas, 12
Celtic pie, 216
Cereals, 10
Ceredigion
  cawl, 60
  kidneys, 171
Cheddar, Welsh farmhouse, with chicken
    breasts, 129
Cheese, 10, 14, 326–31
  Abernant, 331
  Acorn, 329
  and apple potato cake, 203
  Blaenwaun Moorland, 331
  Caerphilly, 11, 326, 327, 331
  Caldey Island, 331
  Cardigan, 329
  Caron goatsmilk, 331
  Caws Cenarth, 329
  Cheddar, 129, 327
  ewe's milk, 327
  farmhouse, 129, 327
  Llanboidy, 331
  Llangloffan, 331
  Maes Mawr, 331
  Maesllyn, 331

making of, 328–9
Merlin, 331
moorland goat's, 327
Nevern Dairies, 329
Pant-y-Gawn Farm goat's, 330
Pantllyn, 331
Pauper's, 331
Pen y Bont, 331
Pencarreg, 331
Plas Dairy Farm, 330
pudding, 214
sauce, pumpkin in, 230
Skirrid ewe's milk, 330
soft, 327
Teifi, 330
Tyn Grug, 331
Waugron, 331
Welsh farmhouse Cheddar, 129
Cheesy leek tarts, 212
Chicken
 Abergavenny, 131
 breasts with Welsh farmhouse Cheddar, 129
 Dark Age, 139
 how to joint, 17–18
 kebabs with blackberry sauce, 133
 pie, Welsh, 149
 with plums, 127
Chinese spring onions, 186
Chocolate mousse, The richest, 257
Chutney
 apple and mint, 318
 in the raw, 315
 pear, 317
Cider, 325
 rosemary, ginger and honey, with roast leg
  of lamb, 188
Cockles
 and bacon pie, 74
 and pasta, 97
 deep-fried, 46
Cookery procedures, 17–19
Cooking foil, 22
Court bouillon, 40
Crab
 and laver parcels, 48
 devilled, 95
Cream, 10
Croffta leeks, 228
Crumble, plum, 239
Crunchy bran fingers, 303
Curd cakes, 239

Dabs, Tenby, 82
Daffodil
 as emblem, 12
 as food, 9
Dairy produce, 10, 13, 14, 240, 326–31
Damsons with rabbit, 147
Dark Age chicken, 139
Deep-fried cockles, 46
Devilled crab, 95
Dowset, 253
Dresser, Welsh, 12
Dried fruits, 239
Duck
 roast with honey, lemon and mint sauce, 137

salt, 11, 118, 145
Dumplings, oatmeal, 209

Eggs, Anglesey, 44
Elderflower cream with summer berries, 241

Faggots, 15, 154, 166
Fairing pies, 12
Farmhouse oatcakes, 296
Fennel sauce with hake, 87
Fish, 9, 11, 71–3
 bard's dish, 93
 fresh, 72
 how to bone, 18
Fisherman's pie, 111
Flame, how to, 22
Foil, use in cooking, 22
Fool(s)
 fruit, 239
 ginger and apple, 263
Fruit
 and berries, 11
 boozy, 313
 fools, 239

Game, 118
Garlic
 sauce with sea bass, 107
 to crush a clove, 19
 wild, with pan-fried pork, 183
Gelatine, how to use, 22
Geranium water ice, 251
Gin, scallops in, 109
Ginger
 and apple fool, 263
 and honey cake, 299
 and honey syllabub, 248
 and plum jam, 321
 honey, cider and rosemary with roast leg of
  lamb, 188
Gingerbread, 288
Give me Yesterday, 323
Glamorgan sausages, 199, 233
Goat's cheese, 327
 fried, with rhubarb sauce, 66
Good Cookery (1867), 11, 154, 276, 327
Goose with apple stuffing, 143
Gooseberry
 and rhubarb jam, 321
 pie with elderflower, 239
 turnover, 249
Gower cockle and bacon pie, 74
Granny Griffiths' cawl, 56, 324
Grapefruit with mead, 45
Green pancakes, 58
Green salad with honey dressing, 235
Griddle (bakestone), 10, 239–40
 cakes and soup, diet of, 10
Grilling, 154
Guinea fowl, stuffed, 123

Hake with fennel sauce, 87
Ham(s)
 and beef loaf, 190
 of mutton, 11
 Pencarreg, 168

Hare in red wine, 135
Harvest
  broth, 12
  cake, 12
  hot pot, 170
Hazelnut, lemon and honey mousse, 246
Herbs, 239
  and flavourings, 9, 14, 15
  beef and mushroom pie, 160
  as medicine, 324
  mushroom and spinach mould, 223
Herrings
  marinated with apple and lemon yogurt, 62
  stuffed, 86
History of Welsh cookery, 9–15
Honey, 14, 325
  and ginger cake, 299
  and ginger syllabub, 248
  and mustard sauce, as marinade for salmon,
    38
  buns, 286
  cider, rosemary and ginger with roast leg of
    lamb, 188
  dressing, 200, 235
  dressing with green salad, 235
  fruit tea, iced, 310
  garlic and white wine sauce with rack of
    Welsh lamb, 177
  hazelnut and lemon mousse, 246
  lemon and mint sauce, with roast duck, 137
  spareribs in, 185
Hospitality of the Welsh, 11–12
Hot pot, harvest, 170
Hot scallop mousse with prawn sauce, 32
How Green was my Valley, 15, 239

Ice cream, 240
Iced honey fruit tea, 310

Jam
  making, 14
  plum and ginger, 321
  rhubarb and gooseberry, 321
Junket, 239

Katt pie, 191
Kidney(s)
  and steak cobbler, 156
  Ceredigion, 171

Lamb, 153
  and laverbread roll, 175
  and mint sausages, 180
  chops, Welsh, with sweet herbs, 187
  fillets of, stuffed with spinach and brown
    bread, 173
  rack of, with lavender, 195
  rack of Welsh, with a honey, garlic and
    white wine sauce, 177
  roast leg of, with ginger, honey, cider and
    rosemary, 188
  to bone a loin and best end of neck, 18
  to prepare a best end of loin to roast as a
    rack, 19
  Welsh, 14, 325
Lamburgers, 179

Lavender with rack of lamb, 195
Laver (porphyra umbilicalis, edible seaweed), 14
  and crab parcels, 48
Laverbread
  and lamb roll, 175
  cakes with bacon, 50
  mussel and tomato tart, 113
Leek(s)
  and bacon pudding, 162
  and carrot medley, 201
  and potato pie, 222
  and potato soup, 52
  and salmon soup, chilled, 40
  as emblem, 12–13
  cheesy tarts, 212
  Croffta, 228
  trout cooked in, 101
Lemon
  and apple yogurt as marinade for herrings,
    62
  berry pudding, 267
  honey and hazelnut mousse, 246
Lentil and parsnip pots, 207
Llanddarog Fair cakes, 12, 298
Llandeilo loin of pork, 193
Llanover, Lady, 11, 118, 154, 276, 327
Llewellyn, Richard, 15, 239, 275
Loin of pork Llandeilo, 193
Love spoons, origin of, 16

Mackerel
  Aberaeron, 99
  smoked, 11
  with oranges, 103
Mayonnaise, to make, 20–21
Mead, 14, 311, 325
  with grapefruit, 45
Methods of cooking meat, 154–5
Michaelmas cawl, 12
Milk, 327–8
Mint and apple chutney, 318
Mint leaves, sugared, 45
Monmouth pudding, 239, 244
Mousse
  hazelnut, lemon and honey, 246
  richest chocolate, 257
  scallop, 32
Mulled wine, 312
Mushroom(s)
  and Caerphilly pancake, 218
  herb and beef pie, 160
  spinach and herb mould, 223
  wild, 14
  wild with pasta, 210
Mussel(s)
  broth, 36
  pâté, 28
  with parsley and tomato sauce, 84
Mustard and honey sauce as marinade for
  salmon, 38
Mutton, leg of, 153

Notes on the recipes, 23–4

Oatcakes, 10, 276
  farmhouse, 296

Oatmeal
  dumplings, 209
  whisky cream, 255
Oats, cooking with, 276
Offal, 155
Onion cake, 221
Oranges with mackerel, 103
Oven temperatures, 24

Pancakes, 10, 239, 240
  apple, 265
  Caerphilly and mushroom, 218
  green, 58
  spiced apple, 240
  spinach, 231
  tips on making perfect, 21
Parry Jones, David, 276
Parsley
  and tomato sauce with mussels, 84
  broth, 30
  pie, 64
Parsnip
  and lentil pots, 207
  pie, 205
Pasta
  and cockles, 97
  with wild mushrooms, 210
Pasteurized milk, 327–8
Pastry, 239–40
  rough puff, 119
  savoury choux, 160
  shortcrust, 191–2
  suet, 162
  to prepare, 20–21
Pâté, mussel, 28
Pear chutney, 317
Pembroke sauce with sewin, 91
Pembrokeshire duck roast with whinberry
  sauce, 125
Pencarreg ham, 168
Pheasant and apples, 121
Pickled pork, 181
Pies
  beef, mushroom and herb, 160
  Celtic, 216
  Fairing, 12
  fisherman's, 111
  gooseberry with elderflower, 239
  Gower cockle and bacon, 74
  Katt, 191
  leek and potato, 222
  parsley, 64
  parsnip, 205
  pigeon, 119
  Templeton Fair Katt, 12
  venison, 141
  Welsh chicken, 149
Pigeon pie, 119
Pigs, 153–4
Pikelets, 285
Plum(s)
  and ginger jam, 321
  crumble, 239
  with chicken, 127
Pork, 153–4
  loin of, Llandeilo, 193

pan-fried with wild garlic, 183
  pickled, 181
  St Tudno, 158
Potato
  and leek pie, 222
  and leek soup, 52
Poultry, 117–18
Prawn(s)
  and yogurt cheese with sorrel parcels, 54
  pan-fried with sorrel mayonnaise, 34
  sauce with hot scallop mousse, 32
Preserves, 14, 309, 313–22
Puddings, 239–40
  bacon and leek, 162
  berry lemon, 267
  blackcurrant layer, 258
  cheese, 214
  Monmouth, 239, 244
  Snowdonia, 239, 270
  Sunday rice, 239, 243
  Welsh apple, 261
  Welsh bread and butter, 272
Pumpkin in cheese sauce, 230
Punchnep, 199–200, 202

Rabbit with damsons, 147
Rack of Welsh lamb with a honey, garlic and
  white wine sauce, 177
Recipes:
  adapted to current tastes, 13
  notes on, 23–4
Red wine, hare in, 135
Redcurrant and apple sauce, 319
Regional recipes, 12
Rhubarb
  and gooseberry jam, 321
  sauce with fried goat's milk cheese, 66
Rice
  fruity, 131-2
  pudding, Sunday, 239, 243
  nutty, 134
  saffron, 110
Richest chocolate mousse, The, 257
Rosemary, ginger, honey and cider with roast
  leg of lamb, 188
Roulade of fresh salmon, with an avocado and
  smoked salmon filling, 105
Roux, 19

Saffron rice, 110
St Tudno pork, 158
Salad(s), 200
  green, with honey dressing, 235
Salmon, 14
  and leek soup, chilled, 40
  and Teifi sauce, 11, 78
  marinated with honey and mustard sauce,
  38
  roulade of fresh, with an avocado and
  smoked salmon filling, 105
Salt duck, 11, 118, 145
Samphire (edible seaweed), 14
  with scallops, 76
Sauces
  blackberry, 133
  cheese, 230

fennel, 87
garlic, 107
honey and mustard, 38
honey, garlic and white wine, 177
honey, lemon and mint, 137
parsley and tomato, 84
Pembroke, 91
prawn, 32
redcurrant and apple, 319
rhubarb, 66
sorrel, 89
sour cream, 59
Teifi, 11, 78
to thicken, 19–20
whinberry, 125
Sausages, Glamorgan, 199, 233
Scallop(s)
  in gin, 109
  mousse, hot, with prawn sauce, 32
  with samphire, 76
Scones, 276
  Caerphilly, 300
Sea bass with garlic sauce, 107
Sea trout (sewin), 14, 71–2
Seaweed
  laver, lettuce-leaf type, 14
  samphire, 14
Sethyd, strawberry, 269
Sewin (sea trout), 14, 71–2
  with Pembroke sauce, 91
Shearing cakes, 12
Shell shortbread, 295
Shellfish, 9, 13, 14, 15, 71
Shortbread, shell, 295
Skate, with sorrel sauce, 89
Snowdonia pudding, 239, 270
Sorrel
  mayonnaise with pan-fried prawns, 34
  parcels with yogurt cheese and prawns, 54
  sauce with skate, 89
  soup, 31
Soup(s)
  and griddle cakes, diet of, 10
  chilled salmon and leek, 40
  leek and potato, 52
  sorrel, 31
Sour cream
  broad beans in, 220
  sauce, 59
Spareribs in honey, 185
Spiced apple pancakes, 240
Spinach
  and brown bread stuffing for fillets of lamb,
    173
  herb and mushroom mould, 223
  pancakes, 231
Sponge, wholemeal, 290
Spring onions, Chinese, 186
Steak and kidney cobbler, 156
Stoneground wholemeal bread, 293
Strawberry sethyd, 269
Sugar thermometer, 320
Sugared mint leaves, 45
Summer berries with elderflower cream, 241

Sunday rice pudding, 243
Sweet herbs with Welsh lamb chops, 187
Syllabub, 239
  ginger and honey, 248

Tarts
  blackberry and apple, 239
  cheesy leek, 212
  laverbread, mussel and tomato, 113
Tea, iced honey fruit, 310
Teifi sauce and salmon, 11, 78
Teisen Lap, 292
Templeton Fair Katt pies, 12
Tenby dabs, 82
Threshing cake, 12
Tinfoil, to use, 22
Tinker's cakes, 12, 281
Tomato(es)
  and parsley sauce with mussels, 84
  to peel, 21
Traditions, 13
Trout
  cooked in leeks, 101
  filled with watercress, 80
Turnover, gooseberry, 249

Vines, 9
  leaves, stuffed, 225
Vegetables, 10, 11, 199–200
Vegetarians, 199–200
Venison pie, 141
Viniculture, 324–5

Watercress-filled trout, 80
Water ice, geranium, 251
Welsh
  apple pudding, 261
  Bouillabaisse, 42
  bread and butter pudding, 272
  cakes, 280
  chicken pie, 149
  dresser, 12
  history of Welsh cookery, 9–15
  hospitality, 11–12
  lamb, 14, 325
  rarebit, 227, 327
  whisky, 9
Welsh Country Upbringing, 276
Welsh Folk Museum, St Fagans, 11, 16
Whinberry sauce with roast Pembrokeshire
    duck, 125
Whisky
  oatmeal cream, 255
  Welsh, 9
Wholemeal sponge, 290
Wild Wales, 153
William James, 323
Wines
  making, 14
  mulled, 312
  Welsh, 11, 323, 324–5

Yogurt cheese and prawns with sorrel parcels,
    54